97 Things Every Engineering Manager Should Know

Camille Fournier

Beijing · Boston · Farnham · Sebastopol · Tokyo

97 Things Every Engineering Manager Should Know

by Camille Fournier

Published by O'Reilly Media, Inc., 1005 Gravenstein Highway North, Sebastopol, CA 95472.

O'Reilly books may be purchased for educational, business, or sales promotional use. Online editions are also available for most titles (*http://oreilly.com*). For more information, contact our corporate/institutional sales department: 800-998-9938 or *corporate@oreilly.com*.

Acquisitions Editor: Melissa Duffield	**Indexer:** Angela Howard
Developmental Editor: Alicia Young	**Interior Designer:** Monica Kamsvaag
Production Editor: Nan Barber	**Cover Designer:** Randy Comer
Copyeditor: Octal Publishing, LLC	**Illustrator:** Rebecca Demarest
Proofreader: Dan Fauxsmith	

December 2019:   First Edition

Revision History for the First Edition
2019-11-20:   First Release
2021-03-26:   Second Release

See *http://oreilly.com/catalog/errata.csp?isbn=9781492050902* for release details.

978-1-492-05090-2

LSI

Table of Contents

Advanced PeopleOps— One-on-One Retrospectives

Marcus Blankenship

Carmen's heart sunk as she looked at her calendar. Back-to-back one-on-one meetings filled her day, overflowing into the next.

"Ugh…maybe I could call in sick. Or make up an excuse to work from home. My boss wouldn't care. My team would be thrilled to skip them."

"It's not too late, you can still call in sick," she thought as she stood in the Starbucks line, "But then what kind of boss would you be? It sucks, and everyone hates it, but you have to do it."

"Sheesh, what are we gonna talk about? I guess I'll just ask people what they're working on this week, and hopefully, I can get each one done in five minutes. Oh! Or maybe we could do them in small groups! That would take soooooo much less time."

"I'd better order an extra-large coffee with quad shots…I'm going to need it."

Apply What You Already Know

I'm going to share a head-smackingly simple lesson that has served me well. Ready?

Make every fourth one-on-one meeting a retrospective to discuss improvements to your one-on-ones.

This is similar to a sprint retrospective, and you can use the same format. The point of a sprint retrospective is for the team to improve. The point of this retrospective is to improve your one-on-ones, making them more valuable for both of you.

That's it. Go do it.

But, if you need a nudge…

Here are five steps to help you start:

1. Let each team member know that the next one-on-one meeting will be used to discuss your one-on-one meetings.
2. Ask them to write down what's working for them, what's not working, and ideas for change. You will do the same.
3. During the meeting, discuss what you both wrote, just like in a normal retrospective.
4. Brainstorm a list together of possible actions that will improve the meetings.
5. Choose a few actions, again together, to try for the next three meetings, and then discuss them in your next one-on-one retrospective.

Simply start talking about your one-on-ones with the other person and discuss how they could be better.

What If You're Not the Boss?

What can you do to improve a one-on-one that is inflicted on you? Here are some simple, but maybe not easy, ways to broach the subject with your boss:

- Forward this article to your boss, with a note that you'd like to try one-on-one retrospectives.
- In your next one-on-one meeting, ask if you can take a few minutes to discuss how the meeting can be improved.
- Brainstorm a retro-style "glad-sad-mad" list about the meeting and bring it to the next meeting.
- Ask your boss what the real goal of the meeting is and whether they feel this format is working.
- Let your boss know that the current meeting format frustrates you and that you'd like to discuss changing it.
- Tell your boss the way you feel about your one-on-one meetings, and then ask how they feel about them.

Talk about what's really happening. Stop pretending that your one-on-ones are great, or that they can't be changed, or that you're benefiting from them as much as you could be.

Best case: the meetings will improve, your boss will appreciate your initiative, and you'll do better work.

Worst case: your boss says, "No, things are fine as is. How dare you suggest they could be improved? Just give me your status update."

(If the worst case happens, you have bigger problems than crummy one-on-one meetings.)

What Kinds of Things Can Be Changed About a 1:1 Meeting?

It's easy to fall into a rut with your one-on-one meetings, like an old married couple can fall into a pattern about how they spend Friday nights. Here are 10 things about your one-on-ones that you could change but might not have considered. (There are surely many more, but this should get your creative juices flowing.)

- How often you meet (it doesn't have to be the same frequency with each person)
- What time you meet (it doesn't have to always be at the same time)
- Who runs the meeting (how could you take turns running the meeting?)
- Where you meet (consider a walking meeting or a breakfast meeting)
- What preparation both of you do for the meeting (try more, or less, prep)
- The agenda for the meeting
- The goal of the meeting
- The length of the meeting
- The communication medium (face-to-face, telephone, Slack, Skype, etc.)
- What you could combine it with (a meal, a walk, a commute, etc.)

Do You Wait Too Long to Consider a Change?

When I begin to feel in a rut, I ask myself some questions. In particular, I ask whether my current practices still fit with my current situation or reality. Often, I find that this one question allows me to be more agile, more creative, and less judging. It lets me see new possibilities that I'd been missing.

For example, if I were dreading my one-on-ones, I might ask questions such as these:

- What is my secret goal for these meetings?
- What is my spoken goal for them?
- What is the other person's goal for them?

- What is the company's goal for them?
- What would happen if we stopped doing them?
- What parts are valuable to me and which feel like a waste?
- What parts are valuable to them and which feel like a waste?
- What is the least we could do and still have a valuable one-on-one meeting?
- What do we need to add, subtract, change?

Grandma's Ham

Albert Einstein summed it up pretty well when he said, "The important thing is not to stop questioning."

Jane asked her mother, "Why do you cut the ends off the ham before baking it?"

Her mother answered, "Because that's how your grandma taught me to do it. Ask Grandma."

When Jane asked her Grandma, she replied, "My roasting pan was small, so I had to cut the ends off the ham to fit it in the pan."

It's difficult to question the status quo.

Not just because you want to avoid looking dumb or rocking the boat or breaking tradition, but because you might not realize there's a question to ask.

New possibilities are wonderful. New choices and options do exist about how we work together. New possibilities bring hope that the future doesn't need to be like the past and that we can grow and improve.

What a great thought!

Answer These 10 Questions to Understand Whether You're a Good Manager

Cate Huston

Something I struggled with as a new manager was finding a sense of accomplishment. It's difficult to find the right success metrics upon which to judge our work because our output is to make the team better. Without success metrics beyond the team's improvement, though, it can be easy to feel like you're just riding a wave of good people doing good work without contributing anything yourself.

Some managers deal with this feeling by seeing their success metric as being available to their teams 24/7 (unsustainable) or by counting lines of code (which would be like editors focusing on the number of words they wrote themselves—absurd). Some embrace the performance of management without understanding the underlying motivations. They "perform good manager" in one-on-one meetings, standup meetings, and feedback cycles, but it doesn't really make them feel accomplished, and it's difficult to put a finger on why.

To that end, I've compiled a list of signs that I look for in managers on my teams that suggest they're doing a good job.

Can You Take a Week Off?

There's nothing like a week off (or more!) to show which of your activities has the *most* impact. When you come back, pay attention to what you find. What's surprising to you? What comes up in your one-on-one meetings? What did people miss? What did they not need you for?

Can Problems Be Handled Without You?

This is huge—you'll never get away from using constant availability as your metric if every emergency must come to you. Ensuring that everyone on the team feels a sense of responsibility and ownership, and having a clear Directly Responsible Individual (DRI) is key.

Does Your Team Deliver Consistently?

Delivery is a trailing indicator for a healthy team, but it *is* an indicator. Healthy teams ship, consistently, and keep shipping over time. We all have projects that become unexpectedly complex, and every individual one might have a reasonable explanation, but if you look at the overall picture, is the team delivering more often than not?

Do People Tell You What They Think?

One thing that we all must get used to in leadership is people being less candid with us. We need to make ourselves available explicitly to people who don't want to presume to seek us out (these are important people to listen to; otherwise, you just hear the loudest voices).

It's also important to note *how* people give you critical feedback. Do they wait until it's something they are really frustrated by? Or is it an ongoing conversation? Will people tell you what they are worried or insecure about? Will they share what they notice is going on around you?

Do People on the Team Treat Each Other Well?

Effective teams are inclusive teams. As a leader, it's on you to cultivate a respectful environment on your team, and to make it clear that you will not tolerate discriminatory words or behavior. This is the minimum. Beyond that, you can set some values around reward and advancement that make it clear that success on your team is something that happens interdependently, not as a competition.

Is the Team Self-Improving?

Self-improving teams critique and iterate and change things as a part of their process. They're not afraid to discuss what worked and what didn't, make suggestions, and try changes *knowing that some of the changes they make will fail.*

These teams get better over time with less and less intervention from you. It can be difficult to get teams reflecting on what went right and wrong with a project because this process is scary (and the first few times might be quite rough). But getting to a place where these "postmortems" are a matter of course is the outcome of a self-improving team.

Can You Give People Who Report to You Meaningful, In-Depth Feedback?

The way I think about feedback is this: feedback is someone's work reflected back to them, in a way that helps them take pride in their accomplishments and makes actionable the places where they can improve. This means having enough insight into their work, accomplishments, and struggles to be able to do that. A lot of that feedback happens as we go, but at most, every six months I make a point to get some (qualitative or quantitative) feedback from team members that I can use to put together a bigger picture of how someone is doing.

What Kinds of Things Can You Delegate?

Do you feel like you can hand off pieces of work or problems to people on your team? Are those projects growing bigger over time? Maybe you started by giving people tasks, but over time, you want to be able to give them broader problems to own. This allows you to take on more.

If you manage managers and you don't have people to whom you can hand stuff off, you will drown. It's just not possible to operate effectively at that scale without the shock absorption of people being able to take things off your plate and handle them. If you don't have it, you will need to build it, *because it will only get worse over time.*

Who Is Taking on Bigger Roles?

As the team grows, there's more opportunity—and more need—for people to step up. Delegation flows down: pushing things onto the managers forces them to push things onto people on their teams, and this is how we grow new leaders.

As much as we might adore everyone on our team and want to keep them together, having a strong team means that sometimes people's best path for success lies outside of it. It's our job as managers to help them toward it. It's a sign of success when people from our teams go to other teams and take on more responsibility there.

Can You Take on Work Outside of Your Immediate Scope?

Having our own teams in order, and strong support within them, makes it possible for us to provide more support to those above and around us. What could you take on that would most help your boss? Your peers? Can the scope of your work get bigger over time?

Do Your Peers Value Your Perspective and Come to You for Advice?

Every organization has its own unique set of quirks, and the people who best understand the stress under which we operate are our peers. In a functional and collaborative environment, who respects whom in a peer group says a lot. Pay attention to the topics people seem to value your opinion on. It shows what they notice—which are often the things we most take for granted.

Avoiding Traps in Manager READMEs

Camille Fournier

Manager READMEs are a popular idea in engineering management circles. The concept is roughly that you, the manager, are writing a README similar to one that you might find attached to a codebase—a "user guide" for your team. That README can contain everything from the deeply personal, such as a manager's stated values and personality quirks, to the more mundane, such as expectations for one-on-one meetings, communication standards for the team, and ways to contact them.

Insofar as they stick to the mundane, manager READMEs are somewhat useful. Writing down how and when you expect your team to communicate with you can be great, especially for managers running distributed teams where there isn't the obvious in-office synchronization. If you can be explicit about your expectations for a new employee's first 90 days, or how you prefer to be contacted outside of work hours, when you want status updates, and how you run your meetings, that is all useful information to have written down.

But writer beware! If you decide to stray into the personal, the personality quirks, and core values, you are entering dangerous territory. Although you might be writing these down in the hopes of building trust between you and your team, you are just as likely to erode and undermine trust with these writings as you are to build it.

How do these documents erode trust? First, they encourage the practice of listing out personality quirks in order to help people understand your behavior. *I suck at niceties. I get heated sometimes in discussions. I don't give praise very much.* Well, so what? If you know you have foibles/quirks that you want to change about yourself, *do the work*. Don't put them out there for your team to praise you for the intention to do the work—just do it. And even though you get to decide which of your foibles/quirks/challenges you will or will not change about yourself, as a manager, it is on you to make your team effective, and that might require changing some things about yourself that you don't want to change.

Writing these down feels good, like you've been honest and vulnerable, which means that no one can be surprised when you behave badly—after all, you warned them! But it does not excuse these bad behaviors, and it certainly does not take the sting away when someone feels shut down by your rudeness or unhappy from a lack of positive feedback. Please skip this section. Keep your bad behaviors to yourself, and hold yourself accountable for their impact.

Second, when it comes to sharing your values and your behaviors, you probably do not know yourself as well as you think. If you've gone through any coaching or therapy, what you learn over time is how difficult it is to be 100% honest about yourself and your motivations. If you've gone through very little of that, you are likely in some degree of denial about your behaviors and how accurately they reflect your conscious beliefs.

So what happens when you put out this declaration of self-awareness then behave in such a way as to contradict the person you claimed to be? You damage your credibility. You damage the trust you might otherwise have built with your team. And you make it more difficult for people to call you on your hypocrisy, because they know that you don't see yourself this way. It is incredibly difficult to tell someone that something they believe about themselves enough to publicly declare is, in fact, not true. It's hard to tell your partner that, it's hard to tell your friends that, and it's basically impossible to tell your boss that.

It doesn't matter that you've encouraged your team to give you feedback: you have a huge power differential over a person who reports to you. Most people have had managers who claim they want feedback and then react by shutting down, blaming, or otherwise making it clear that maybe they do want *some* feedback, *sometimes*, but not *this* feedback, not at *this* time, not in *this* way. Your team is not likely to give you the feedback you need to honestly assess and correct your behaviors, and it's not their job to do so.

If you want to build trust, you do that by showing up, talking to them both individually and as a team, and behaving in an ethical, reliable manner. Over and over and over again. You don't get it from writing a document about how you deserve their trust. Manager READMEs are not a shortcut.

Building Effective Roadmaps

Travis Donia

Effective roadmaps help a cross-functional organization make deliberate choices about a product's development. Whether you're writing a roadmap or reading one, you have a stake in making sure the roadmap answers the questions on which you need stakeholders to provide consensus. Here are some questions that good roadmaps answer.

What Impact Will This Have on Users?

Outcomes are more important than outputs. When building a product roadmap, it helps to be explicit about the types of behavior that you intend to encourage. In Agile development, this intent is codified in user stories: *As a* [type of user], *I want to* [activity]. In other development methodologies, use cases perform a similar function. Regardless of how it works in your organization, the goal is the same: put the user first and speak to the behavioral impact that you want to create, not just the outputs that must be built.

How Will We Measure Impact?

It also helps to know how you will measure that impact—especially if your team will need to implement the metrics. Work with stakeholders to get consensus at the outset on how you'll measure and have them ballpark the impact they expect a feature to have. Document your hypotheses. Prior to implementation, those estimates will provide a gut check for the roadmap— is this outcome realistic? Post-release, comparing the hypotheses with actuals will help create a feedback loop that will improve your ability to estimate impact in future releases.

What Are Our Strategic Objectives?

As an engineering leader, understanding the strategic objectives that underlie a series of releases will help you guide your team on the abstractions that will be long lasting, the expectations the business holds on scale requirements, and where new interfaces will need to exist between teams and services. It's also a good way to talk about timing and the order of operations. Even if these objectives are documented elsewhere, explicitly referencing the Objectives and Key Results (OKRs) you're building toward will help make sure your plans are consistent with your goals.

What Are We Willing to Give Up?

There's a wide range of features you *could* build; the roadmap is intended to capture those that you *will* build. Out of a broad product opportunity space, the roadmap articulates the specific choices that have been made. Sometimes, that strategy is most evident in the reflection of what you're willing to give up. To do this, consider the opportunity costs—the features you're not pursuing—as a way to make explicit the product values you are expressing. For example, if your market places a high value on privacy, there are a number of social features that you won't be able to pursue. By highlighting those trade-offs, you can expose the strategy underneath them.

What Are We Testing and What Mistakes Are We Comfortable Making?

Another important function of a roadmap is to reveal the places where there's uncertainty. Uncertainty is part of the process; if the correct answer was obvious, someone else would have built it already. For your team, flagging the areas of the implementation under active testing is important for managing the level of attention you invest in an implementation.

Similarly, not every step will take you forward. If you knew that you were making a mistake, you probably wouldn't make it. With that in mind, effective roadmaps should also flag irreversible steps and make sure there's consensus among stakeholders that the risk is worth it.

How Will These Features Roll Out?

Effective roadmaps help coordinate the release by indicating how features will be introduced to users. The marketing team will probably appreciate having visibility into the work for which it will need capacity. Assume the same is true for the other teams you work with; use the roadmap to identify those dependencies upfront.

By covering the plan for releasing features in the roadmap, it will help build alignment and de-risk a release. For instance, if you know that a feature has open questions and is being actively tested, you can recommend giving preview access to a small set of customers and collecting their feedback before turning it on for everyone. Anticipating this in the roadmap will make it significantly easier to implement feature flags during development and will provide the other teams you're working with the flexibility they can use to answer the open questions.

Good roadmaps create momentum as more teams' needs are represented. That doesn't happen by accident. Someone in the organization is working to ensure that your product's roadmap spurs the coordination that makes the product better with every release. Even if you're not responsible for crafting the roadmap, you can make it more effective by helping to ensure that it's answering the right questions.

Thank you to Stephanie Wai for reading and editing drafts of this essay.

Busy Isn't Better

Colleen Johnson

As managers, we are asked to spend a lot of our time making sure that our people stay busy. Busy producing new features, busy fixing bugs, busy addressing technical debt, busy figuring out what will keep us busy next. We track our team's capacity in spreadsheets down to the hour, trying to account for how much of each day is spent in meetings or forecast who will become available next. There's pressure on us to make sure that no one is idle. Ever.

Some of this pressure comes from appearance. We don't want it to seem like our team isn't pulling its weight or contributing its fair share. Some of this pressure also comes from the need to plan and estimate. We are always looking to account for each hour of the day so that we can accurately predict our team's output. Unfortunately, the closer we get to maxing out our capacity, the worse our output gets.

Development requires research time. I'm willing to guess that every engineer on your team cannot crank out code all day without having to look up examples or investigate their approach. This isn't a bad thing! You want to make sure that they have time to explore best practices, understand new libraries, and dig in to new technologies. Without this time, your team will be making guesses and introducing defects.

Development requires the ability to respond to unplanned work. As much as we try to isolate our teams from interruptions, they are big part of the job. This is not just dealing with production issues or hotfixes, but also answering questions or participating in team meetings.

Give your team members slack in their day to respond to things as they come up. Without this space, your team will constantly be stopping work on something to address an urgent request or high priority.

Development requires a sustainable pace. When the amount of work your team has in progress changes wildly from day to day, we create chaos. The team sees a giant pile of work ahead of it and rushes to get through it in order to hit a date or milestone. Teams need to work at a pace that doesn't give them anxiety to come to work each day. Without this flow, your team will be stressed out always trying to rush to "catch up."

When we manage our team toward 100% of its capacity, the reality looks more like 120% or more. Our teams end up working in a state of being constantly overburdened without the time to do its job well. Team members feel rushed and unhappy with the quality of what they are producing and end up filling in their free time to do the learning that work will not allow. We add more to this imbalance when new requests come to the team, taking its attention away from its work yet again and moving the target on what is most important to complete.

Our goal in all of this is creating a consistent flow of work for our team. Flow from an engineering team's perspective means the time that it takes for work to move through our system. Your role as the team's manager is to build an environment in which flow can exist. Create space for your team. Give it the room to breathe; room to learn; room to respond. Provide it with room to enjoy what it does. You'll have a happier team that is more excited to contribute high-quality code and can absorb new requests without smashing a printer.

Career Conversations as an Engineering Manager

Raquel Vélez

Whether your direct report is ambitious, oblivious, or anywhere in between, your job is to help them navigate their careers. It's irrelevant where they are in their careers (e.g., early, middle, or advanced), it's in everyone's best interest to grow in a continuously challenging environment.

That said, it's not your job to create or fully outline their career paths; note that you are a guide, *not* a mapmaker. Your goal is to develop a trusting relationship with your reports, understanding what they want for themselves and giving them the opportunities they need to succeed.

For your first career conversation with a given report, it's essential that you two get on the same page as quickly as possible. Even if you've been working together for years, it's possible that you don't know them and their motivations as well as you think you do. The sooner you identify the gaps, the sooner you can work on closing them.

The following is my framework for having productive career conversations:

First, mention in a one-on-one that you'd like to talk about their careers. Give them the following homework:

- If your organization has a career path, ask them to review it and identify where they think they are on the path. If your organization does not have a career path, ask them to consider what level they think they are at and why. (And then get to work on building a career path.)

- Ask them to answer the following questions:

  — Do you have goals or a timeline in which you would like to reach the next level?

  — Are there areas that you've identified as growth areas for yourself?

— Given the work that you have done so far, what would you like to keep doing? Stop doing? Start doing?

— Have you started compiling the work you've been doing? If so, is it up to date?

In the career conversation one-on-one, compare answers to the first homework exercise. If you're in agreement, great! Move on to the next step. If you disagree, it's time to have a deeper discussion about why you each believe you are correct. *This is management, uncomfortable though it might be.*

After you have reached a mutual understanding of where your report is in their careers, set that as their baseline. Now move on to the second homework exercise.

The first question is how you will gauge their understanding of how careers work. Compare their timeline with the reality of your organization. This is a great time to set expectations and avoid conflict down the road.

The second question allows the engineer to think critically about their own growth. It's important that everyone have agency over their careers, but sometimes people expect their managers to do the work for them. This is your opportunity to set the boundary: they are in charge of their careers; you are in charge of paving the way so that they can succeed. If you have also identified areas of growth for them, this is a great time to discuss it with them.

The third question gives you, the manager, a better sense of what kind of work your report likes to do. Although we all have to do "grunt work" from time to time, people do tend to be more effective in their roles when they are enjoying themselves. Use this question as an opportunity to better understand what sorts of projects your report will excel in as well as growth areas into which you can push them. This way, you can do resource planning with a purpose—you're getting the work done while also helping your reports grow!

Finally, I always ask my reports to keep track of the work they've done to date. It should include the project, relevant tasks, timeline, and impact to the team/organization/company. The purpose of this document is three-fold:

1. Brains are squishy and often forget details big and small. If it's written down and shared, it's less likely that key elements of a promotion packet will be forgotten.

2. You can't guarantee that you will always be their manager, and having a document that can stay with the individual engineer means that onboarding a new manager will be easier than having to start from scratch. (This is especially helpful in fast-growing companies, where an individual contributor might go through more than three or four managers in a single year!)

3. Finally, there's no guarantee that an employee will stay at a company for their entire careers (and is increasingly uncommon to do so). As such, an accomplishments document will be helpful when filling out resumes and helping the individual get their next position, regardless of what company they head to next.

That done, set a regular cadence to check in on career paths. Whether it's monthly or quarterly (yearly doesn't seem to be regular enough; weekly isn't productive), ask the same questions and check in to see whether folks are moving along the path. If you're both invested in the process, you'll see regular, incremental improvement, with the direct report in charge of their own destiny.

Career Development for Startup Engineers

Josh Tyler

In the early days of a startup, not too many people are concerned with "career development." They're too busy trying to keep the lights on and hit the next milestone, which can have life-or-death consequences for the company.

But after people have been with the company for a year or two and things have stabilized to the point that they can think more long term about their career, they will. They want to continue growing and are looking for a path. (Side note: hopefully you hired people who want to grow.) If they don't see that path within your team, they will look outside.

Here are some ways to provide career development:

- Share the opportunity to work on larger projects
- Create more specialization
- Hire experienced mentors
- Invest in training and classes

If your company is growing, so are the size and scope of your projects. Share the opportunity to lead these projects, especially with your top performers. You don't need to do it all. In fact, you shouldn't. Is there an upcoming effort to add language support and internationalize the product? Perfect, ask a promising senior engineer if they can lead it. As Laszlo Bock, author of *Work Rules!* and former senior vice president of people operations at Google says (*https://oreil.ly/7_XpR*), "You want to give people a little more freedom than you're comfortable with."

Early stage startups typically don't require specialization. Rather, they require generalists who can do a bit of everything to solve the most pressing questions each day. If you only have one or two engineers in a web startup, they better know a bit about the backend, the frontend, the database, and server ops.

As the team grows, though, more specialization is required. The level of server ops knowledge to handle 1,000 requests per day is very different than the level required for 10,000 requests per second—even with virtualization in Amazon. It's the same for other technical areas. At some point, a generalist isn't enough.

The good news is that most people on your team probably want to be (or already are) an expert in some area. They see specialization as the opportunity to work on the most difficult and most impactful technical problems. (By contrast, a dedicated generalist is probably more motivated by working on the hardest *business* problems.) Indeed, some people will be able to develop specialized skills out of their own initiative. Some, however, will need help, which is where hiring and training can make a difference.

One of the biggest hiring shifts you will see with your team is the need to hire into more specialized roles, for the same reasons as I just mentioned. Your projects are becoming more complicated and require more specific expertise. Your search for a "software engineer" turns into "frontend engineer," "backend engineer," "site reliability engineer," "systems engineer," and so on—not to mention all of the different levels of possible experience (such as senior, staff, or principal).

Creating specialized roles actually makes hiring easier in a couple ways. First, it allows you to post more roles. This might sound simplistic, but circulating more unique job listings will increase the overall number of people you hear from.

Second, it allows you to more precisely target your recruiting, which makes it easier to source and screen people based on their skills and experience. A search for engineers with at least five years of experience and knowledge of React and TypeScript will turn up fewer results than simply "frontend developer," but the ones you find are more likely to be a match. To borrow terminology from the field of information retrieval, you can improve your precision without much loss in recall.

Finally, you can promote career development through investment in training programs. Offering an educational assistance program is a great start, but on its own isn't enough. People need to use it. Some people have the drive to find programs on their own, but others need more help and encouragement. Either way, some commitment is required. If you make the courses free for all employees, they'll sign up quickly but rarely complete them. They need to have some kind of vested interest, which could be as simple as getting manager approval, thereby creating an emotional commitment.

It might take a while to see the benefits of learning programs in your team's work, but remember—now you're playing the long game.

Communicating with Executives

Travis Kimmel

Early in my career as an engineering manager, I would become frustrated when upper management seemingly brushed off challenges in engineering or asked me questions that seemed irrelevant. My perception was that the non-technical side of the business was out of touch or even at odds against technical initiatives—to the detriment of the business as I saw it.

In hindsight this all makes a bit more sense. As organizations grow, an inevitable amount of complexity is introduced. The sheer variety of projects, people, and responsibilities on the minds of those at the top can be overwhelming.

In my tenure as CEO, I've learned how to navigate a constant stream of demands competing for my attention, where it is not possible to unpack complex topics in real time. I now recognize the problem was probably two-fold. First, senior leaders faced raw, demanding items and were often fighting fires where mine wasn't the priority. Second, I probably didn't communicate in a way that got their attention.

Here are a few tips for communicating with and presenting to executives that have held true for me in the years since joining the ranks of management:

The granularity of your conversations should scale to match your company size
On the smallest teams, you might spend time talking about specific tasks. A bit larger, and you're talking about sprints or collections of tasks. At hundreds or thousands of employees, you're likely talking in terms of broad themes of work or long-term initiatives and resource allocation. As the company scales, you'll be expected to be more independent when it comes to managing tactical concerns, and focusing your communication on larger themes as the company grows (while continuing to handle

lower-level items autonomously) is an important signal that you as a leader are scaling with the company.

Push information up frequently without being asked to do so
Depending on your role, you might not be speaking directly to senior leadership on a regular basis. Your manager might be, however, so it's helpful to consider them as a communication channel. Keep your manager in the loop proactively even when things are going well. It's easy to slip into firefighting mode, but pushing bursty updates about things being on track is often just as valuable, and it gives you an opportunity to showcase the work your team is doing.

The patterns for communicating upward are almost the inverse of communication with your team
Team-centric communication is often about fostering autonomy, and overcommunication at that layer can be distracting or come off as condescending. Upward communication is the opposite: rarely will you run into a problem overcommunicating, and the larger the company, the more bursty updates serve as valuable reminders to your stakeholders about everything currently in play.

Tell them what you're going to tell them, tell them, and then tell them what you told them
It's a natural tendency to want to build the story before finally landing on the thesis. That might work for a TED talk, but it doesn't really work in an executive setting. Tell them what you're going to tell them. "We'd like to spend three weeks paying down technical debt. Today I'm going to discuss why we'd like to do that and what we're focusing on, and I would like to leave with a 'go' or a 'no-go' decision." Do that and then provide a summary of what you told them (ideally in written form) and restate the goals of your communication with a concrete ask or information about when the next update will happen.

Think of it as a three-step process that does the following:

1. I'm telling you about X because of Y.

2. Here are the details on X.

3. I need you to do Z so that I can accomplish X because of Y.

This pattern is very effective with executives; it helps frontload your message with information about why the conversation is important as well as what you need in terms of executive backing and mandate:

Write the narrative first

Before you begin thinking about the presentation, write a narrative explaining your argument and recommendation. Organize your thoughts in writing first as if your manager were going to review it. This will help identify gaps in your understanding of the problem and give you a template for following up in writing after the conversation. Done well, it will help you sufficiently consider and address the various perspectives and constraints of the problem—and after you've prepped at this level you will rarely be caught out when you're advocating to a larger audience.

Creating a presentation is much easier after the narrative is written. I like to write out the narrative, trim the fat, and build slides around it.

Don't be evasive, and prepare for detours

Senior leaders will frequently pierce into areas that they see as potential problems, sometimes uncovering gaps in the presenter's understanding of the problem. These unexpected questions can quickly derail the entire presentation toward a thread of follow-up questions as they dig even further. Presentations to executives that take an unexpected turn are common; their experience has helped tune their radar for knowing when to dive in further.

Along the same vein, answer their questions directly. Executive radar quickly picks up on evasive answers, so err on the side of "I don't know but I'll find out" as opposed to vamping. It's generally fine not to know something, and if you take detailed notes and follow up after this will almost always work to your advantage.

Numbers are the language of business

Use data to explain the current constraints, context, or progress of the problem. If you don't provide data and instead skip to the analysis, you're relying on trust and persuasion to get the information, guidance, or resources that you need. Executives are by nature very results oriented, so make sure anything you propose is coupled with data that will allow them to process the problem themselves in a "show your work" fashion.

The ideal outcome of a meeting is one where everyone leaves with shared understanding of the path ahead, and the surest way to get there is inclusion of the data that led you to your own conclusions.

Lead with the ask

Go into the meeting with a clear goal. Start the meeting by explicitly framing the goal, and then return to the ask at the end of the meeting. Executive time is precious, so make sure to be respectful of that by having a clear outcome for the meeting. It's generally better to be a little over-ambitious in your ask than it is to meander about without obvious action items.

Communication as Craft

Patrick Pena

We all maintain a mental model of our craft, the skills and measurements we use to know that we are effective at our jobs. There's a change to that definition that happens when you transition into a leadership role. The skills that made you an effective engineer—your technical abilities—are not the ones you need to be an effective leader. The way that you provide value is through your ability to have impact on your team instead of your individual productivity. To be effective in leading people, you need to develop your communication skills and abilities. Here are some key concepts that should help you in your journey.

What we say is not always what others hear
> We all have filters through which we process information. I can say something in a one-on-one on Monday, and by Tuesday I'm hearing I said something slightly different from someone else on my team. The more time that goes by, the more the message changes. If you want your message to be consistently heard, try delivering it through different medium and more frequently than you think is needed.

Meet people where they are
> There's two parts to this one. You should consider how they think and process information. How you form a meaningful connection. Everyone also has preferences around how they like to communicate. Some people prefer Slack, some prefer email, others prefer in-person conversations. It is your job to learn what they prefer and to meet them there. Remember, you are responsible for learning how to effectively communicate with your team.

The impact of your words matters more than your intent
> In a poor attempt to rush out a message, I asked my team to meet me in a conference room in five minutes. It was for a celebration, but I left that part out of my message. The impact of my words put a temporary load of stress on my team that I could have avoided. Take the extra second, the extra review, or a second set of eyes to make sure that what you intend to say is what you are conveying to your audience.

(Re)Frame for positivity

Every communication you make is a chance to shape and reshape people's perspectives. Your communication influences your team more than you can imagine. They take cues from you. You can talk about mistakes as learning opportunities. You can remind people of all the progress that they have made. Highlight ways people are growing and stretching skills. Set the tone that you want your team to have.

There is value in silence

We have all experienced that awkward pause in a conversation. You've asked a question, only to be met by empty space. You wait a second or two, which feels like an eternity, and then you try to fill it. Remember that not every answer or thought comes straight away. Instead of filling the silence, give someone space. Show that you value whatever they have to say, and you're willing to wait to hear it.

Connect "The What" to "The Why"

Jeremy Wight

As an engineering leader, you have many projects and tasks demanding your time; some you want to do, and some you need to do. In the midst of planning meetings, scoping and estimating, researching, designing specifications, meeting with cross-functional leaders, one-on-ones, performance reviews, status updates, and more, there is much to fill an engineering managers time. With all of that, it's easy to lose focus on your highest-leverage activity:

> The highest leverage activity of an engineering manager is making sure that the engineers who report to them have clarity, alignment, and ultimately understand "The Why" to "The What."

The What is the work in which the team engages on a daily basis. Clarity gives people an understanding of how they accomplish the root of the request. Alignment ensures that what they are working on fits into the broader scope of work that the team and business are executing upon. But *The Why* allows an individual to truly understand the impact of their work. The Why affords them the depth of insight needed to create truly innovative solutions and serves as a wellspring of empathetic user-driven motivation.

Given the amazing impact of connecting *The What* with *The Why*, how come it is so often overlooked? Busyness and lack of awareness. Managers are often so overwhelmed that it is easy to forget. An engineering manager gathers a great deal of context through all of the meetings, conversations, user interviews, and the breadth of data that flows through them, and it is easy to overlook the fact that much of this never makes it to the engineers. It is also easy to assume that everyone remembers the words that a manager shares. It has been said that it takes seven times hearing the same message for it to stick. This means that a manager must constantly repeat the core message that they want their team members to retain. Due to this, keeping people consistently aware of The Why can be extremely difficult, especially in the high pace culture of startups. How do you overcome this?

Constantly Reinforce *The Why*

At least weekly, if not more often, write a message to your team helping to connect *The What* to *The Why*. Whether they are changing work focus or continuing on the same path, by helping the team to reconnect what they are doing to why it is so impactful for users, it presents the opportunity to intrinsically reignite the value of their work.

Here are a couple of examples of things that you might share to different groups to connect *The Why* to *The What*.

To the full company in a general channel:

> Good morning team!
>
> So excited for all the value that we are going to imagine, create, and deliver to our current and future users! It's going to be a great week!
>
> What you do today matters! Giddyup!

To the engineering team in a team channel:

> I just want to remind you of how impactful [this improvement] is to our current and future users. During two recent interviews, both Sam and Julie commented specifically on how painful that experience was before I even showed them the prototype! When I mentioned that we were already underway with this and that we would complete it soon, they were so excited! What you are doing today matters!

Directly to an individual working on a difficult bug:

> Thank you so much for persevering through this bug fix, I know it's been a difficult one to overcome. What you are doing here matters. This isn't merely a random bug off the backlog. When I followed up with Grace last week to let her know that we were working on this, she was so excited. It's been something that has kept her from being able to use [this feature]. So just remember as you continue your progress, Grace and others are excited to use it!

It's so easy for an engineering manager to focus on merely what they need to do, don't forget to engage in the highest-leverage activity, connecting *The What* to *The Why*.

Continuous Kindness

Nik Knight

Individuals and interactions over processes and tools
    —The Agile Manifesto

We all know this, right?

Individuals and interactions cover many things—pair programming, daily standups, retrospectives, banter on Slack, random chats at the water-cooler. All that good stuff that we know greases the wheels and unblocks us when we're stuck. The times we get this right, things just seem to work so much better and we get into that lovely state of *flow*. Simple, yeah?

Only it's not, is it? My Twitter feed, conversations with friends and colleagues, the abundance of blogs, articles and five-point methods all over the internet—even books like this one—tell me that this stuff isn't simple and that we haven't got this basic principle down in a large number of our workplaces. Work doesn't just flow; we are frustrated by conflicting priorities, overwhelmed by too much work in progress, hampered by unsuitable procedures, and struggling with tools that aren't the silver bullet we thought (hoped) they would be.

And yet, shiny new tools, process improvements, scalable frameworks, and trendy methodologies get a hell of a lot of airspace, considering it is interactions between individuals that we know deep down is the real priority. So why is implementing a funky new ChatOps app so much more appealing than improving our working relationships?

The topic of "kindness" came up in a recent conversation, and it got me thinking about how a lack of kindness and related behaviors — compassion, assumption of good faith, empathy, trust — is what really holds us back when we're talking about individuals and interactions. We lack trust in other teams, so we add in more process instead of fixing the broken relationship. We assume people in different parts of our value chain don't understand us rather than explaining our difficulties to them. We get defensive when someone reacts negatively to a situation instead of asking ourselves why they are struggling with it. Instead, we unleash our inner badass and have the fight, or we retreat and hide and hope it all goes away, or we grumble and moan to our close circle, or whatever our own brand of counterproductive behavior happens to be.

None of these are easy patterns to break—they are often deeply ingrained habits, perhaps reinforced by an unhealthy team or company culture, or driven because we *just don't have time for this crap*. It takes conscious effort to practice kindness—continuous kindness—so that whatever the situation, we're ready to step back and ask ourselves what is *really* going on here, and what *we* could do to change it. (It's not always possible, of course—sometimes people are just being jerks, but this genuinely happens a lot less often than you'd think. I promise.) The really interesting thing is that there is enormous power in being kind—it's difficult to fight someone who is being patient, seeking to understand you, and demonstrably trying to help. At the same time, it's much easier to start building trust in that person, get a good feeling about working with them, begin to generate that elusive state of flow. It's also pretty infectious; one person in a positive frame of mind will likely approach other situations more constructively, improving the interactions with other individuals, continuing to spread the kindness wider.

Being badass will undoubtedly get you so far—let's face it, we all know someone who often seems to get away with it, at least in the short term. But being kindass will get you—and everyone else—so much further.

Culture Is What You Do When the Unexpected Happens

Ines Sombra

We all want to work in diverse and inclusive places. We want to be a part of companies with "good culture." But how can you tell what that means and whether your company has one? You might think that looking at your company values (if you have them) is a good indicator, but values are rarely polemic, and they tend to be aspirational in nature. I'm not trying to belittle how important the introspection needed to derive company values is; I'm merely pointing out that stating a goal does not necessarily make it true.

I believe that culture is what happens when what we want to believe about ourselves is challenged. Culture is what we do when we get things wrong, when we witness a violation of trust, or when we stay silent when an inappropriate comment is said in our presence. Culture is made when we catch ourselves acting in opposition to our values.

Note that good intentions don't matter when it comes to building an organization's culture. Even well-meaning people can have bad days, get tired, cranky, or say things that could have been phrased better. But here is the challenge: everyone in an organization is enforcing and creating its culture, and none more so than its leaders.

It's your responsibility as a leader to understand that your actions can normalize a bad behavior or model a good one. You can recite your company values all you want, but if at the first sight of a confrontation your first reaction is to caveat, excuse it, or wish it away your inability to act informs everyone in your organization what your culture really is. To reiterate, it's about how you act when something happens. For example; if your reaction when people elevate problems or concerns to you is to chastise the reporter for not being more positive, congratulations, you have created a culture of spin and nontruths in which Pollyanna thinking is encouraged.

On the other hand, as a member of an organization, it's your responsibility to expect your leaders' actions to match what the organization likes to tell itself. When incidents happen (if you are in a position to do so), elevate concerns, report wrongdoings, and call out acts of cognitive dissonance. And if you are not a member of an underrepresented group, you have a heightened responsibility to use your privilege and demand better. This is how you do your part in creating a good company culture.

As job seekers, what can we do when the barometer of a "good" place is what an organization does when incidents occur, but this information is not available to us when we are interviewing? Our only option is to use our interview time wisely and ask probing questions to help get a feel for dissonance. For example: What behavior will not be tolerated in the organization? What are the protocols in place for reporting and handling of incidents? Are they anonymous? Are they documented? How often are they used? How is retaliation prevented? When was the last time a complaint was made, and are you satisfied with the way you handled it? What do you do as a leader when you realize you handled an escalation poorly?

It's tempting to believe that company culture is a static thing that can be checked off after it's on the website. Unfortunately, this is not the case. Building a good culture is a daily endeavor, and there are no shortcuts. As leaders it's our responsibility to look critically at our own behavior and ask ourselves how our shortcomings and blind spots shape the culture of our organizations.

So, to summarize:

- As a leader: it's your responsibility to embody and enforce your organization's values. Don't allow yourself to fall complacent. Your intentions are irrelevant; it's your actions that determine what kind of culture you create.
- As an employee: your behavior matters. Hold your leaders and peers accountable, especially if you are in a privileged position.
- As a job seeker: carefully evaluate a new place before joining. Ask uncomfortable questions, interview members of senior leadership, backchannel the place with your network. In short: trust, voice expectations, and verify.

Dealing with Uncertainty

Mathias Meyer

As a manager, you make decisions—lots of them. Many of them are small, usually quick and easy to make. There might be frameworks in place at your company that help you. For instance, when someone comes and asks you for a raise, a career and salary framework guides you through the process. Finding a yes or no answer and a good explanation is simple enough in those cases.

However, there are many decisions for which you'll be faced with imperfect information. Your view as an engineering manager is limited. Given the many parties that you interact with every day, you have many perspectives to take into account. Some of these will be conflicting, even opposing. Others will contain only a shred of the real picture.

You can delegate decision making to your team as much as possible. But you won't prevent the most uncomfortable decisions from landing on your (virtual) desk at some point.

It's easy to become stuck in these situations because you don't know how to balance the different perspective. You want to be sure that you've considered all perspectives. You want the solution to address all concerns equally. You want to talk to one more person.

Every manager (including me!) has been in this position at some point, and they can very much relate to how you feel. Making decisions in the face of an increasing amount of uncertainty can be terrifying. The higher up you move in your management career, the more uncertainty you'll be faced with. Information will be sparse, and it will be limited in detail.

Here's the flip side that every manager also understands: you're afraid to make a decision. You're afraid to make a decision that your team won't like. You're afraid the team disagrees. You're afraid that you're making the wrong decision and that you'll be exposed as not knowing what you're doing.

Making decisions with imperfect information is never easy. You're asked to predict a future that you know nothing about based on very little knowledge. But not making one will lead to your team not knowing what to do or where to go. Eventually, the team will burn out and leave.

As difficult as this is, you'll need to get used to having to make these kinds of decisions. Some folks will defer these questions to their boss, asking them to make the call in their stead. This can work in smaller teams. But it means that you're not doing your job.

It's tempting to think that you always want to make the correct decision. But I offer a subtly different take: it's important to make a good decision, not always the correct one. A good decision is one that you're making for the right reasons. It's not a decision that everyone must like or agree with.

How do you get there? Here's a little framework that can guide you through the process:

Start defining the problems and goals
Any decision that doesn't have a good set of goals and problem definitions attached to it will likely not get the buy-in you might be hoping for. There are decisions for which this isn't possible due to confidentiality reasons. But for most decisions, be clear on the goals.

This helps avoid bikeshedding, where people argue about the implementation or a detail rather than first reaching agreement on whether they really need a shed.

Collect information from multiple sources
Talk to several people in your company to get a fair overview of what people think about the problem at hand. Don't stretch it out for eternity though. Set yourself a time limit or list out the people who you think would have the strongest opinions and would be affected the most.

Outline the options
Outlining more than one option that you've considered in your decision making makes it clear to people that you've tried to make a fair decision that considers multiple angles, including theirs.

Be cognizant of the risks
Think about what consequences the decision might have and what risks you associate with it. This is a good way to go beyond your fears and gut feeling and really think about the best and the worst that could happen, and anything in between.

Consider doing experiments instead of making decisions

Decisions seem more difficult to make because they tend to appear valid for an infinite amount of time. You can reduce this by considering a decision as an experiment that expires after a period of time. This could be one month, or three, or six. After that time, you'll revisit the decision to see whether it's turned out the way you thought.

Define Your Culture Before It Defines Itself

Mike Pappas

In school, I studied physics and applied mathematics. I spent a long time thinking about formulae and systems, analyzing data, and generally trying to quantify anything in sight.

I tend to bring that attitude into how I think about leading a company. Metrics are important, both to discover strengths and weaknesses and to communicate the state of things.

Culture naturally resists quantitative metrics. (Not to say metrics don't exist —there are a few—but none without fairly obvious gaps.) Because of this, I dismissed the importance of culture when I was still in school and merely speculating about what working at a company would be like.

Fast forward to today, and I haven't really learned much to help me quantify the importance of culture. But nonetheless, I've been convinced.

Culture is really, really important.

What do I mean when I say culture? It's a bit fuzzy, but here's how I think about it:

> A company's product is the *what*. Their customers are the *why*. Their employees are the *who*. Culture is the *how*.

This is a pretty large claim. There's a lot in the "how" that might not traditionally be considered culture. But ultimately, culture is about people, and that's what all questions of "how" boil down to: how do the people in the company operate?

The fact that culture is inherently fuzzy makes it crucial to define clearly what yours is all about. This probably sounds obvious, but I've seen far too many companies end up using something like the following:

We're world-class technologists excited to work on world-changing problems. We care deeply for one another and are united by our desire to make the world a better place.

Now tell me, how much have you really learned from that? And, what's more, what kinds of employees are being selected for by a paragraph like this?

In information theory, information is defined as, roughly, the degree to which one's uncertainty is reduced when they receive it. So, given that definition, my problem with paragraphs like those you just read is that they convey almost no actual information.

This is bad for two reasons. First, this nondescription will fail to separate your company from the pack—and you need to be different to succeed. But, even more dangerously, the risk here is that, by effectively opting out of defining your culture, you're leaving your actual culture up to chance.

With language like this, which doesn't offend or raise disagreements with anybody but also conveys no information, you're likely to find a scattered set of candidates, with very different expectations, coming into your organization. They might all be great in their own ways, but without shared expectations, they'll inevitably clash, and the aspects that eventually win out to become part of your culture will be decided simply by which random types of people join your company earlier on.

If you believe as I do that a good culture can be the difference between success and failure, this should terrify you. And the only way to avoid it is to define your culture at the outset—and do it in a way that conveys information. This means defying someone's expectations—which means there will be people out there who disagree.

It's OK to say, "You're a great candidate but not a good fit for our culture!" That's not a value judgement of a candidate. Companies do have different cultures, and often in ways that meaningfully affect someone's happiness. Some people just want to crush on difficult problems and are totally fine working 12-hour days. Other people deliver the best results not through 12-hour days but through shorter work days allowing for more rest and inspiration. It would be nice to be able to accept any candidates, and give them each the experience best suited for them, but the reality is that this can't always happen.

Your culture definitely needs to be able to accommodate certain kinds of differences from yourself—no company will succeed without a diversity of ideas and backgrounds—but if there's a real, meaningful culture difference, it's crucial to be able to detect, explain, and act on it.

The bottom line is simple: until you can crisply imagine turning away a world-class candidate because they don't match the culture you're building, you haven't yet defined your culture at all.

Delivering Feedback

Jennifer Dyni

Delivering feedback—a valuable skill for any team member—is one of those things that has not come naturally to me.

I started my career thinking that all it took to be good at sharing appreciations or criticisms was to simply state my perspective out loud. (I'm from Jersey: direct is good.) As it turns out, literally spewing out my thoughts and ideas didn't always go very well—or at least not the way I expected it to. My attempts to help influence up, down, and sideways were rarely sunshine and daisies and much more often eye rolls and terse "sure, whatever" blow offs. I also had some spectacular failures where the things I said quickly led coworkers to get visibly angry and tell me off for my insensitivity to their situation.

Clearly, I did a lot of learning what not to do by experiencing it firsthand.

To grow as a leader, I've spent a lot of time exploring and trying different tools and techniques that help me deliver feedback more effectively. Following is some of what has helped me become more successful.

Start with Frameworks

There are many great resources on how to start a conversation with teams or individuals. They map out templates for a variety of situations—for example, appreciation, confrontation, delegation—and I use them to help me map out my opening statement clearly and concisely.

One of the frameworks I use often is called "Continue and Consider":

- If I want to help encourage someone or help them recognize a strength, I kick off my discussion with phrases like "keep repeating" or "be confident with more" with [specific thing I see as a strength] and follow up with examples of the behavior or actions I observed personally that I perceive as kicking butt and taking names.

- When I want to help someone recognize a challenge that I feel is holding them back or needs more attention, I use phrases like "consider changing" or "you can improve your effectiveness" [specific thing I see as an area to grow] and then also support that with examples where I've observed them struggle.
- I also try to include a question after my statements, so that I'm inviting the person to respond and we start a conversation about how things might go differently moving forward.

The start of a "continue" discussion might look like this:

Hey, Ryan. I wanted to give you some feedback about the UI code review you led yesterday with our team. I hope you continue to take the initiative to help our team own the quality of our code, including walking through how to use tools to assess code complexity and run analyses on test coverage. I appreciate that you helped the team walk through refactoring recent UI pull requests without calling out names, helping the team learn without making individuals, especially some of our junior developers, feel bad. How did you think it went?

A "consider" conversation might begin like:

Hannah, I wanted to give you some feedback about the component you've been building for our new feature. When the component was pulled into testing, I noticed that it wasn't integrating shared design libraries and now it will need to be reworked. Consider changing your story analysis process to research or get feedback from other team members about what you might be able to reuse before you start coding.

Some other resources I keep going back to if I'm looking for phrases or questions to reach out with feedback include the following:

- Susan Scott's Fierce Conversations (*https://oreil.ly/oeo6T*)
- Lyssa Adkin's Coaching Agile Teams (*https://oreil.ly/iW2SW*)
- Kerry Patterson and Joseph Grenny's Crucial Conversations (*https://oreil.ly/Ehyjv*)

Attune with Improv

The nonverbal cues I'm communicating during conversations are just as important as the words.

To help me recognize when my natural style might not support my message, I've learned a lot about attuning my delivery as well as my listening with improv techniques. I like using the game "Mirror, Mirror" to stretch my powers of detection and reflection. I find an improv buddy, and then we take turns practicing with different scenarios (from happy situations like winning the lottery to frustrating events like losing our keys) and mirroring the eye contact, hand gestures, and facial expressions our improv buddy is communicating. We then debrief on what we saw—what groups of positive or negative signals we used to interpret what the other person's point of view is and how open or closed they are to the conversation.

Follow Up

There's no such thing as a silver bullet, single perfect feedback conversation. When I'm asking someone to change—even when that change is to do more of a good thing—people often need time to process. I do my best to make it easy for team members to have multiple follow up conversations where they can ask deeper questions about what's expected. What's the urgency? What training or tools do they need? Who else can they connect with for coaching or mentoring? Making myself available to others might look like scheduled or impromptu one on one meetings. Grabbing coffee. A walk around our office campus.

The Results

These tools and techniques have definitely propelled me along my professional journey, helping me progress in my career from individual contributor, to sometimes project/people leader, to full-time engineering team owner. I'm less likely to open mouth, insert foot, especially when I take time to try new techniques in a safe environment. For example, although it seems silly to practice a framework, it helps to role play and try it out a few times so that when you need to use it to start a conversation at work, the word choices feel and sound natural, not scripted (in comparison, try using the "exactly by the template" word choice next time you give feedback to your significant other, who will likely then totally call out that you're clearly up to something).

Developing Communication Patterns

Travis Donia

> *Organizations which design systems are constrained to produce designs which are copies of the communication structures of these organizations.*
> —*Conway's Law, Melvin Conway*

Your job as a manager is to help your team work together effectively. Because the challenge is bigger than any one person, what your team ships will reflect the communication that happens. By developing communication patterns within and around your team, you'll improve what you ship. Here are some ideas on how to begin:

Be a good listener

First, you need to understand what communication patterns are established, so look for the conversations that are already happening. Who is talking to whom, and what about? This will take time. At the beginning, the team won't automatically trust you and might be guarded. Respect that. To build trust, you'll need to be present whenever you're asked for and prove yourself as an active, empathetic, and useful listener. As you build trust, you'll be let in to more conversations. The same is true for communication outside your team. As you work with other parts of your company, you'll identify the conversations you have a stake in, and you can earn the trust to be invited in the future.

Look ahead

You can further earn the team's trust and make it more efficient by anticipating the questions it will have. For instance, wherever your team members' work overlaps, they will need to be aligned on how their work will interface. Junior team members are not always going to plan for that, and there's a risk of wasted effort if an agreed-upon interface isn't defined early enough. By anticipating that, you can ensure that they're communicating with one another early enough in the process to build toward the same goal.

Be a hub

There are only so many questions you can answer, so it's important to learn to route questions to others. For instance, maybe it's better for a member of your team to chat with a PM directly: the PM might be more familiar with the implementation and could answer more of the team's questions. This is a powerful tool, but use it with care. Not everyone will love answering questions, and even for those who do, there's still a limit to the number of questions one person can answer.

Provide visibility

Your job is more than just handling questions; you've have a mandate from the wider organization and direction that you need to give the team. You're responsible for providing visibility to that mandate and its related workstreams. Smart people often work better when they know *why* something is important, so connect the dots between day-to-day work and the big picture when new requests are made. How does fixing a bug improve someone's life or grow the business? Help the team understand where it fits in within the company and where the company fits in within the world. Equally important is helping the company understand the strengths and value of your team. Visibility runs both ways.

Protect your team's time

An endless stream of meetings, chats, and emails consumes valuable time; the code will not write itself. It's just as important to help your team focus so that it has time to do work. It's usually worth asking yourself—and others—is this a good use of time? One of the easiest ways you can make the team more productive is by finding ways to ensure that communication happens without requiring team members to break their flow. This often is why standups happen at the beginning of the day—it means less time lost context switching. "No meeting Tuesdays" is the same idea.

Find the question behind the question

As you grow as a leader, you will be brought into ambiguous situations, and it will become more difficult to know what you can share. The correct answer might not be obvious, and there will be reasons why you cannot share everything. Resist the urge to let this be a reason to depersonalize your relationships or to ask the team to "just trust me." Instead, use those moments to empathize. Listen hard and understand the question behind the question. You might not be able to give the team the sensitive information it's asking for, but you can earn trust by demonstrating that you understand team members' concerns.

As your team places more trust in you, you'll find yourself cc'd on more emails and drawn into more conversations. You'll be asked to provide context more often. You'll be brought problems and given the opportunity to help edit and focus the communication that's happening. Notice the outcomes of the conversations that happen when you're not in the room. These are all signs that you're establishing communication patterns, and that's one of the most important things we can do as managers.

Thank you to Stephanie Wai for reading and editing drafts of this essay.

Distributed Teams Are Founded on Explicit Communication Channels

Juan Pablo Buriticá

All teams past a certain size become distributed. It could be across rooms, floors, buildings or cities. If you manage a team in a company that is growing fast, you will run into this challenge. By being deliberate and explicit about the communication channels used, your teams will be more productive, easier to manage, and able to grow faster. With the increasing popularity of remote work, understanding how to rely on different channels, especially written ones, will also enable you to be better prepared if your team eventually becomes distributed.

The primary benefit of choosing explicit communication types and channels for information is increased productivity. When team members aren't clear on where to find the information, their productivity is affected. They might waste a few hours trying to guess where to find it or, if they're good at asking questions, go around creating unnecessary focus interruptions for their team members. That poorly timed tap on the shoulder or chat app notification during deeply focused programming can be prevented if you are explicit on where and how information can be found.

A good way of reducing interruptions is to choose asynchronous communication channels for nonblocking items and helping team members review them on a cadence. For example, architectural decisions and discussions can begin as long-form documents with an established period of comments, also known as Request For Comments (RFCs). These can eventually be used as onboarding materials or blueprints for future systems. Asynchronous communication is best for situations in which real-time dialog is not necessary. Communicating status, reviewing code, broadcasting organizational changes, and the resolution of questions that are not urgent are well suited for asynchronous channels like collaborative documents, forums, task-tracking tools, and email.

When the real-time exchange of ideas is crucial, it's more appropriate to choose synchronous communication channels like group chats, in-person meetings, or video calls. Grooming a backlog over email, or discussing strategy on a forum or a group chat when different members are busy will probably not lead to a timely outcome. For situations like this, you want to get your teams on a cadence so that they can block their time on the calendar and be present. This is especially important if you are spread across time-zones.

Multichannel chats have gained popularity because they can be used both synchronously and asynchronously. The good use of these tools can have a positive impact on the productivity of a team, but it can also have a detrimental effect if you set an expectation of always being present. Deep focus time is greatly affected when this happens. You can prevent your teams from falling into this behavior if you are explicit about the broadcasting of important information so that team members can disconnect. For example, set up a read-only announcement channel or agree on "quiet hours." Having clear protocols for incident management and conflict resolution can also alleviate the need to be constantly present, in case something important happens.

When you build teams that rely on being in the same location to get access to information, you make it easier for information gaps to proliferate when team members are absent or the team outgrows the space. Information gaps create misalignment, and in turn, you need to spend more time managing communication. By defaulting to written communication channels from the beginning, you make it easier to distribute information that is clear and enables alignment.

One final benefit of investing in explicit communication channels from the beginning is setting up your team for fast growth. When communication practices become standards, events like adding new members to the team are less taxing on the group. For example, if you have a good set of RFCs that cover important past technical decisions and the discussions around them, new hires can understand the trade-offs you had to make. They might even have architectural diagrams or system contracts that are kept up to date with the evolution of your systems. A 90-day onboarding checklist template is another great example. You can use it as an evolving document to which new hires contribute as they navigate their first weeks in your team, making the next hire's experience much better.

Relying on in-person communication in the early days of your team is low friction and convenient, but it can bring your team to a halt if it grows beyond the limitations of physical space. If instead you build a culture of being explicit about the communication types and channels used and lean into written mediums you can build teams that are resilient to fast change. Thanks to the internet, written communications are accessible and aren't subject to the limitations of physical presence, serendipitous encounters by the seltzer machine, or inconvenient taps on the shoulder.

Do Less, Lead More

Katie Womersley

There comes a time for every engineering manager when you just can't do all of the things you need to do. This might be when you first switch to management, and you try to do one-on-ones, lead planning and scoping, figure out performance reviews, and still keep your hands in the code. It comes again later when you first start managing two teams and your workload doubles—even though you do not. It might happen when you need to fill more than one role, or when your startup hits a growth spurt. If you're a leader, this will happen, and it will happen often. If you're ambitious, you want this to happen. Managers level up when they successfully widen their sphere of influence, so you need to learn how to lead more when you can't simply do more.

This is also when most engineering managers fail. You do the logical thing: write up a list of everything that must be done (and you know what must get done; you've been doing it!). You prioritize that list somehow, usually in order of what's on fire right now, and then smash through that list until the wee hours. You sleep too little and repeat the cycle. You get tetchy, make poor decisions, and "clean up yesterday's mess" starts getting added to tomorrow's TODO list. It does not end well.

Big changes call for desperate measures. The mistake here is trying to do everything that must be done, because you think you can do it. You're wrong. Sooner or later, something will slip, and the chances are, it will be something important that never reached urgent status. Instead of letting your failures pick you, you must explicitly choose what you will let fail. *Intentionally not doing certain tasks is a manager super power.* The best leaders learn this early and rely on this skill often.

A common example of needing to choose what to let go so that you don't find yourself accidentally losing sight of something critical occurs when you step up to lead two teams for the first time. This is often the first management step up, and you need to change how you operate because you won't have enough hours to lead both teams in the same way you led your one previous team. To attempt that would mean doing everything badly. Instead, figure out which team really needs to succeed, and which initiatives really need your personal guidance.

If you had to report back to your own manager that one of these teams is off track or one subproject is slipping, what would you rather be sharing bad news about? Use this "bad news test" to identify what you can delegate and who on your team is competent and eager to take on the extra responsibility. For example, you might do shorter one-on-ones or fewer skip-level one-on-ones, and you might delegate leading standups to a senior engineer. Or, you might pause or delegate your project to revamp the engineering onboarding process.

After you've delegated the things that can more safely fail, focus your efforts on the things that (really) can't fail. This is a small subset of the things you think you "must" do. Choose wisely and choose few. Don't let this list expand, or you'll be again making an implicit choice about what will fall through the cracks. Make sure to share what you expect will slip with anyone who will be affected as well as with anyone who might help.

The worst thing you can do here is secretly let things slide, because you're ashamed of having priorities. Priorities are vital! Share openly what your responsibilities and goals are, the outcomes that you are choosing to prioritize, and the changes that you'll make. Tell your stakeholders clearly what has been delegated, deprioritized, or simply won't get done.

Telling people what you're *not* doing achieves two things. First, it builds trust that you made an intentional decision—you have not simply forgotten. Second, and more important, by pairing your own prioritization with delegating these tasks to developing leaders on your team, it creates room for others to level up along with you. The best leaders take what they say no to, and use that as an opportunity to create a growth opportunity for someone else.

If you do this successfully, you'll not only deliver what really matters. You'll also have leveled up your team and scaled yourself by increasing the leadership of those around you. Before you know it, you'll be promoted—and the intense growth cycle will begin again.

Don't Be the S---
Umbrella

Jeff Foster

When I first became an engineering manager, I saw my goal as protecting the team. I'd heroically take the flak from more senior managers, disgruntled salespeople, and field angry questions from support. I'd do everything I could to ensure that the team spent as much time as possible coding. I'd insulate the team from reality, protect them from outside harmful intent and basically just be a s--- umbrella. It's not glamorous work, but it's what a manager does, right?

Not right at all. This is not what an engineering manager should do!

By insulating the team, I was putting myself under tremendous amounts of stress. After a few months, this job wasn't enjoyable any more. There's only so many calls you can take late at night before it takes its toll. It's easy to accept that this is the only way—that's why managers get paid the big bucks, isn't it?

So, what's wrong with being an umbrella?

First, it fails for you, the manager, because you are putting yourself under unnecessary stress. You are not a superhero and eventually all that external pressure is going to adversely affect you.

Second (and far more important), it fails for every single person on your team. By being the umbrella, you are actively harming the team's development. You are shielding the team from the reality of the project and stifling the personal development of team members.

What should you do, instead?

In my opinion, one of the most important things you can do as a manager is be transparent with your team. Don't be an umbrella, be a *context provider*.

At first, this feels counterintuitive. My team is populated by engineers, they don't care about all of these "politics." This isn't true—the days of an engineer putting headphones on and writing code all day are gone. Engineers aren't measured on the number of lines they write, it's all about the business value. Providing the context in which they are operating is the most effective way to help them increase their value to the business and support their personal development.

This isn't about abdicating your responsibilities as a manager. It doesn't mean just acting as a filter. It means that you are constantly providing the team with a realistic understanding of the context they are operating in and involving your team in coming up with solutions.

For example, I remember one time when marketing contacted my team in a fluster because there was a major conference in a few months and it didn't look like we'd get a release done by then. The naive approach to pass this onto the team would be to just let everyone know that we have a deadline and they should type faster (that's how things get shipped quicker, right?). The context provider approach is to invite marketing to talk to the team, help it get a deeper understanding of the problem and collaboratively come up with a better option. For the case I just mentioned, an engineer on the team made the breakthrough by reframing the problem—we don't need to release a new feature, we just need to demo it. The context reframed the problem and the team came up with a better solution.

By being a context provider, you can enable your team to show you their expertise. I'm a firm believer that the best people to make decisions are those closest to the problem. By giving context to the engineers on your team, you're setting them up for success and future development.

In short, don't be a s--- umbrella: provide context, listen, and enable your team to grow.

Don't Elevate the Means Beyond the End

Seth Dobbs

Our industry is rife with trendy technologies such as microservices, serverless, and blockchain, and trendy processes such as Agile and Lean in all of their various forms. Years ago, the trends were EJBs and UML, and before that, shifting to object orientation and having a structured Waterfall were important.

In their time, none of these were bad in and of themselves, but each wave creates the potential for missing the point behind each of these waves and leads to organizations serving the means. This behavior manifests in comments such as "that's a bad requirement because it doesn't fit our architecture" and "that's not Agile!" In fact, we as an industry can become dogmatic around the means as if *that* is our purpose rather than them merely being tools.

For example, I've encountered several organizations with the directive to "implement microservices." The problem is, "not having microservices" isn't a problem, *per se*, nor is microservices a solution in and of itself. It is a tool or a means for solving a problem. This becomes more ironic in organizations that are dogmatic about Agile given that the *Agile Manifesto* is itself a set of principles that among other things eschews dogmatic process.

Not to pick on microservices specifically; this is an architectural approach that provides a ton of value for certain problem spaces, just as EJBs, RPCs, remote SQL, and various other technologies and techniques have in the past. Which is precisely the point; none of these were the final approach to building software, yet each time we as an industry are faced with a new approach, it becomes *the* solution, even though many of us have been around long enough to know things will change again.

Put simply, what does it mean to replatform to microservices? How do we know whether we've done it correctly? In the absence of an actual business problem we're trying to solve, it's hard to actually measure the value of what we've done. Which is why we as technology leaders should embrace the following principle:

Don't elevate the means beyond the end.

In other words, we need to remember that we are solving problems for our business and for our users and that, ultimately, our approaches have value only when they achieve an end.

As an industry, we often have a tendency to elevate the means; learning new technologies is a big reason why many of us are in this field, after all. And sometimes our development teams feel distant from the overall value of the company we work for, so we focus on what we can control to make our lives interesting.

However, I believe that feeling that our development work is well-aligned with the overall success of the companies we work for is a very rewarding feeling and provides the greatest motivation for our teams.

Putting this into practice means understanding that our business needs don't serve our architecture but rather that our architectures enable us to achieve something great.

Each of the approaches mentioned at the start are (or were) good at solving specific problems and were considered the modern approach in their time, but modernizing an architecture in and of itself is not an end. "Modernizing" doesn't give us guidance into how to best leverage microservices or whatever the next wave will be. Understanding the end goals—be it organizational agility, horizontal scalability to minimize downtime at high loads, or some other need, will help us make better decisions on how to approach our work.

If we can understand when we should and shouldn't use new technologies, how they better solve problems than past approaches, and how to apply them to solve problems facing our companies, we will be truly successful.

Don't Look for A Players

Lisa van Gelder

We know that the 10x developer is a myth, and we don't look for Ninjas or Rockstars in our job postings anymore. So why do we still talk about hiring A Players or categorize team members into A, B, or C Players as if their growth or skillset were fixed?

I first came across the term "A Player" at a company that used the Topgrading interview process—tagline "How To Hire, Coach and Keep A Players." The idea is to categorize candidates into A, B, or C Players during the interview process and to hire only A Players. This assumes that skill is fixed and all you need to do is identify it—and heaven help you if you don't weed out the non–A Players before you hire them! In fact, if you don't weed them out during the interview process, it means that you aren't an A Player: "A players hire A players, B players hire C players," as Steve Jobs said.

So why do I have a problem with it? First, it goes against my belief in a *growth mindset* versus *fixed mindset*. Those with a fixed mindset believe that abilities are innate, whereas those with a growth mindset believe people acquire abilities through effort or study. I prefer to invest in my people. There are engineers who, with good coaching and career development, can deliver far more to the team than someone who might have wowed during their interview.

Second, it leaves you wide open to unconscious bias. Only A Players hire A Players? Isn't that a subtle suggestion to interviewers to hire more people like themselves? How diverse are your interviewers? If you're not careful, you'll end up with a monoculture, and your team will be less effective because of it.

I've also come across the term A Players in HR exercises in which you group employees into A, B, or C players—with the idea that you're only meant to invest in your A Players and not waste time on B or C players. This makes me uncomfortable for a different reason. You're asking managers to choose whom they invest their energy in; this has huge potential for unconscious bias. How diverse are your managers? Is it possible they'll see the most potential in people like themselves? Is there any kind of oversight process?

I also believe being an A Player versus B versus C is situational. Someone who is an A Player on one team might be a B player on another team. Someone who is an A Player one week might be a B Player another week due to illness, family circumstances, and so on. Calling someone a B or C player removes all responsibility from the managers of the team. Team doing badly? Must be full of B and C players. It couldn't possibly have anything to do with the managers who didn't give good direction or set clear expectations with the team members, right?

So, companies shouldn't care about the performance of their employees? No, of course they should. But treat skills as something that can be learned and performance as situational, and watch out for unconscious bias.

Don't Just Evaluate Candidates on Skills

Jay Signorello

The penalties for hiring the wrong people can be enormous. So, it's critical that you, as a manager, put a great deal of effort into creating and continuously refining your interview process with the goal of finding exceptional people. In the pursuit of finding great people, your focus areas for evaluating candidates will be one of the most important ways to differentiate between the best and worst candidates.

It's not uncommon for a new manager to focus exclusively on skills required for the position. They craft their tests to determine whether the candidate has knowledge in a particular programming language, framework, and other technical areas. As they begin interviewing, they'll get a false sense of security when they find many people who can't complete the test, thinking that they're doing a good job of filtering out poor candidates. Then, one candidate will come along and breeze right through the test. The manager thinks to themselves, "Wow, this person must be amazing." So, they quickly hire them.

After a month or so on the job, however, the manager receives feedback from their team that this employee is difficult to work with and closed minded. Now the manager has their work cut out for them. They'll need to work with the employee on interpersonal skills and try to align them on the team's values. These rarely change for most people. So, not surprisingly, the employee becomes upset over their manager's feedback. And the problems only grow worse from there.

Our job as managers is to avoid these sorts of problems altogether by putting together a team that works incredibly well together. Team members should play off one another's strengths and weaknesses while also sharing common values. To accomplish this, you'll need to instead focus your evaluations on values, abilities, and skills (in that order).

Values are a person's principles or standards of behavior. For example, a person might value the ability to move quickly or continuously learn new technologies. If your organization is at odds with a candidate's values, there will always be tension in the relationship. So, it's important that your organization defines and documents its own values. Your team should take those values and rank them based on what's most important to their group's particular needs. The more values that are aligned, the higher the likelihood the candidate will excel in the team and organization.

Abilities are the things that come easy to people. Their inherent talents. For example, a person can be detail oriented or, conversely, able to look at the "big picture." Certainly, anyone can be detailed or see things from a higher level. But those who don't have those abilities need to work extra hard to have the same level of quality. Incorrectly evaluating these will result in your time being spent constantly monitoring the consistency of quality for an employee, which is unlikely the best use of your time.

Values and abilities aren't areas you can question a candidate about directly. Imagine asking a candidate whether they value moving quickly. What is the probability they will answer that they value moving slowly? Low. Candidates are unlikely to admit they lack an ability. Worse, some misaligned candidates will tell you that they agree with your values, but will do everything they can after being hired to change them. This will require you as a manager to create tests that evaluate on default behaviors while also assessing their track records. For example, when your organization values continuous learning, you should be asking how they've demonstrated it previously. You could also ask them to share resources they've recently used to gain a new skill. If the candidate has difficulty coming up with examples, it's a big red flag.

It's understandable why managers gravitate toward skills evaluations. They're straightforward to test on. Just remember, though, skills are also the easiest area for an employee to improve upon. Great employees will be excited to take on new learning challenges. All you'll need to do is allocate some time for them to gain those skills, either in projects or through dedicated time. Evaluating on values and abilities is more difficult at the outset, but it pays large dividends in the end, making it worth the extra work.

Engineering Productivity

Camille Fournier

I'm often asked about the characteristics of great engineering managers. This is a question that almost always has a long answer that involves, "Well, she's good at X, and he's good at Y, and then there's Z..." Every management role is slightly different, and a great engineering team will have managers who reflect a set of complementary skill sets (such as operations, people management and coaching, and product focus) that are aligned with what their subgroup most needs.

However, for most of us, there is one characteristic that is not optional or debatable, which is that a great engineering manager is capable of creating a highly productive engineering team. This is one of the distinguishing characteristics of the management side of engineering. Call it what you will — drive for results, goal oriented — if you are not great at getting your team to be productive, this is a critical growth opportunity.

How do I know this is important? Ask any engineering manager at a startup what one of their most dreaded questions is, and they will almost certainly mention "why isn't it done yet?" Engineering productivity is a difficult thing to measure, but most of us know intuitively what it feels like to be on a productive team. We're shipping things, we're focused, we feel like we know what we're doing and why it is important.

So, what are the management skills that are needed to achieve this result? At the first level of management, they look like:

- Breaking down the scope of projects to help your team ship frequently. An eye for the Minimum Viable Product (MVP), for sequencing work, and for predicting likely risks and bottlenecks for project completion are the skills here. This is why I think project management is such an important part of engineering leadership development and why I hate to hand it off to professional project managers for work that doesn't cross teams or organizations.

- Balancing product delivery with sustainable engineering so that you don't end up with code that can't be maintained in the future. The amount you will invest here depends on the future certainty (baby startup? Probably not so much!), but there's a reason we call it "technical debt" and that is because it inevitably comes due, unless you declare bankruptcy.

- Prioritizing, prioritizing, prioritizing. Implicit in the first two skills is the ability to figure out what is important and prioritize it. If you overprioritize shipping, you might get a lot done for a while and then slow down as the debt you've accumulated comes due. Overprioritize sustaining engineering and you don't ship product. You might not start out with these instincts, but they can be developed, so don't be afraid to start making judgment calls now and learning from the results.

Managers who fail in these three areas quickly show why this is such an important skill set. Teams that don't ship are usually disengaged and rarely get the positive feedback of seeing their work come to fruition. Teams that don't ever clean up their tech debt end up burning out from the difficulty of supporting their software and the challenges of building new features. And when teams don't prioritize effectively, they end up burning cycles on things that are ultimately not that important, which often contributes to a sense of purposelessness.

This is not the only thing that is important in engineering management, but without a focus on delivery, you are letting your team down in a critical way. So, while you're learning how to have good one-on-ones, listen to people, create psychologically safe teams, and think about people's careers; don't forget that if your team isn't shipping, you're not doing your job. Nurturing a safe and healthy team helps them do their best work, and helping them identify and deliver that best work is a key part of keeping them healthy.

Like This? Really?

Dave Mangot

I'd been involved in recruiting engineers for much of my career, as a team lead or a senior engineer. But it was not until I became an engineering manager that I truly became horrified by the state of affairs. At many places, when we needed to hire someone, there was a call to the recruiters, who sent tons of cold InMail's to people who might fit the role. There was a stack of potential candidates (if we were lucky) who were invited to come to the office for hours of whiteboard coding and "culture fit" interviews, until we finally settled on a person we were supposed to work with daily for many years. As an engineer at heart, I would have a difficult time thinking of a more poorly designed system. There has to be a better way.

The Funnel

The places where I've worked that recruited well approached the problem from an engineering perspective. What are our inputs and outputs, and how do we use our processing time most efficiently? There can be many criteria for the inputs to our funnel (yes, ultimately recruiting is a sales effort) depending on the engineer we want to attract.

If we want a more diverse pool, we need to make sure our organization is positioned that way by being involved with the appropriate organizations or schools and staffing and supporting our own roles to attract and retain the people we want. If we want people straight out of college, we should have an internship program with a local university. If we want Java programmers, we need to be involved in the Java community. Conferences and meetups are great for this. We want to build the relationships ahead of time, not at the very last moment when they are called for.

As they enter the funnel, we should ask what they're looking for and clearly describe what we're offering. Design the funnel intentionally and make it repeatable. As candidates move through the funnel, we should make sure that each successive interaction brings them closer to a job offer. If they have no chance of success, or new interactions won't bring them closer, we should be respectful of both our time and theirs and exit them from the process.

The Coding Test

If you have a coding test (and yes, if you're hiring engineers, you should), make it something real. If your existing engineers don't write their code on a whiteboard, neither should your prospective ones. Design a test that is applicable to the work they would do. Then, send it home with them. Here are some question that you should consider:

What if they use StackOverflow, or other similar resources?
What if they do? They're normal?

What if someone writes it for them?
You're going to ask them to explain parts of the code, in detail. Why they made decisions. How does a lambda work? If they don't understand the code, that will be very obvious.

What if they cheat?
They might. But, if you begin your relationships assuming the worst about potential employees, instead of treating them like mature adults, you probably have other things to work on in your org besides recruiting.

Closing the Deal

After a candidate has spent all this time with your organization and they've passed all the screening you've carefully devised, it's time to close the deal.

Ultimately, recruiting is a sales job, and we need to know what we're selling. Up until this point, much of the onus of selling is on the candidate. At this point, it's on you. Like any good sales person you need to know the strengths and weaknesses of what you're selling. Above all, you need to be honest about it. Candidates can sense if you're being evasive about the fact that your CTO regularly logs into production hosts and changes configurations. You probably don't need to be forthcoming about *every* blemish, but you shouldn't hide from them either. Honesty is appreciated, with context.

Know the advantages of your organization. Maybe you have a great mentoring program with senior staff. Maybe it's a small, scrappy organization where they could have a lot of impact. Maybe it's a large organization with lots of opportunity for career advancement and restricted stock units (RSUs). Like any good sales person, know to whom you're selling, what they want and need, and how well the product (the job) matches up.

If the candidate is happy with the opportunity you present and they choose a role at your company, congratulations! Now scale it.

Everyone Can Lead with Leverage

Steve Heller

Leverage is an essential aspect of leadership whereby one's own work enables other people's work. Everyone can and should lead.

The glue that binds an effective team and organization is more than the group's collection of skills and knowledge; it consists of the ways we work together, and especially the ways in which we enable one another. When your effort enables and amplifies other people's work, you can be described as a multiplier (*http://multipliersbooks.com/*), and your work exerts leverage. Tech leads and managers constantly enable their teammates; it's their job. For example:

- Projects need planning and ongoing facilitation to progress efficiently.
- Individual contributors (ICs) need coaching to grow and become more effective.
- Teams need leadership to establish a productive environment and modes of collaboration.

How ICs Can Exert Leverage

In addition to team leads and managers, colleagues who build tools and platforms also exert leverage as part of their jobs. All of these roles have natural leverage and enable an organization to operate efficiently.

We can all do work that has leverage, enabling and multiplying the efforts of our colleagues. In fact, it is quite rare that an employee has broad impact or progresses to senior ranks with just expertise (depth) or perspective (breadth) (*https://oreil.ly/pHWSY*), or even both.

What might an individual contributor who is not a project lead do to exert leverage? Here are a few examples:

Abstract
> Develop a tool, process, or method that makes your colleagues', as well as your own, work more efficient. Think of this as establishing a platform upon which colleagues can build.

Generalize
> Generalize the root cause of an issue not only to prevent recurrence of the same problem, but an entire class of related problems, saving colleagues from correcting now-preventable issues.

Share
> When you learn, share your insight with others (*https://oreil.ly/Ykk1K*), multiplying the group's knowledge and making it more likely that your insight will find application.

Architecture
> The ability to step back and see the bigger picture is a valuable skill, both in designing and executing, especially when you can show others specific paths.

Advocate best practices
> These include validating requirements, design methodology, code quality, documentation, testing, success measurement, and reflection.

Communication Is an Essential Tool for Providing Leverage

Effective communication, especially to groups, multiplies knowledge and is an essential task for a leader. This can be done through writing and presenting. Here are some tips:

Know your audience
> Consider what would be the correct technical level and the correct length of time for the particular audience. A given presentation might not be appropriate for two different groups. Radia Perlman (*https://oreil.ly/OQuX_*), an excellent speaker, explains that the ability to speak at any level and for any length of time (with planning) requires both mastery of the material and the communication mode. This requires practice, and it is well worth the investment.

Know your audience

We are often communicating upward. Even though our managers are often familiar with the goals, usually you will be more of an expert in the subject at hand. That's why you're the one talking or writing. Be ready to dive deep because some leaders like asking chained sequences of questions. Ask a colleague if your audience is known for that sort of engagement. Do not hesitate to push back when the discussion wanders too far; time and topic management are appreciated by all.

Know your audience

When you establish a regular channel of communication, a recurring report (upward), an organizational update (downward), and other vehicles, be clear about the goal of the channel, and be sensitive to the amount of time the recipient will typically allocate to each communiqué. It's better to state, "No major updates at this time" than to report unimportant progress.

Know your audience

When communicating with a mixed or broad audience, paint the picture first, and don't hesitate to deliver the conclusion at the start. Templates for meeting reports, conference reports, literature summaries, all while following an executive summary–first style, with a Highlights and Actions structure, permit the rapid digestion of the most salient points while at the same time allowing the reader an easy decision of whether to read on.

Leverage, also known as scope or organizational impact, is commonly reflected in career ladders. For a manager or lead, we speak of scope of control, and for an IC, scope of influence.

To become and effectively serve as a leader, select work that exerts leverage, multiplying the effort of your colleagues. All leaders exert leverage, and doing leveraged work, by definition, makes you a leader.

Fire Them!

Mike Fisher

Fire them! As people managers, we all must deal with personnel who are not performing to our standards or are displaying behaviors that are not aligned with our culture. This sounds very cut and dried, but in most cases it's not. The work that engineers perform is usually multifaceted, and the required competencies are broad. Typically, we need engineers to write code, fix bugs, achieve business results, participate in Agile ceremonies, mentor other engineers, and more. To do these effectively, we need engineers to be great written and verbal communicators, be leaders, be knowledgeable, be collaborative, and be effective, to name just a few competencies.

Often, we are faced with scenarios in which a person is displaying all the correct behaviors but they are not delivering Or, they are achieving their goals but they are doing it in a manner not in line with your culture. Often times some of our most brilliant engineers are curmudgeons who can't work well with others. I call these engineers "brilliant jerks." It's unfortunate for them because much of engineering is team based.

What sounds so clear on paper is often a confusing scenario in which engineering managers become stuck trying to decide whether they have given the engineer enough time to improve or whether a different coaching technique will fix everything. In these scenarios, my guidance to managers is to take action quickly. It's better for the company to begin looking for the replacement and the open position will add some urgency. It's also better for the individual. If they are performing poorly or not behaving well, they should already be aware of it because of all the clear communication you have had with them. These conversations are stressful for everyone, the person giving it and the person receiving it. Keeping the person in this limbo state for a long period of time is super stressful. It is better to let them go so they can find a role more suitable to their skills or a team whose culture is more suited to their behaviors.

But wait, you say! I can't let them go because everyone else will leave, or everything will break, or everyone will hate me. I've seen scores of personnel issues for which managers used these types of excuses to avoid taking action and yet, I have never seen any of these terrible scenarios actually happen. Let's take these one by one and examine the reality:

Everyone will leave

It is true that in many markets engineering unemployment is nearly zero and engineers can find another position almost immediately. However, their departure is still not very likely. Hopefully, most of your engineers love your culture and your mission. They are there in support of something larger than themselves or another individual. The departure of even one key individual usually doesn't undermine the noble mission of the company. Also, unless your team is composed of nothing but junior engineers, they have experienced the frequent departure of friends, colleagues, and managers.

Everything will break

As a manager, one of your many responsibilities is to not allow SPOFs (single points of failure) to exist in the system or on the team. Long before you need to ask someone to leave or someone decides that they want to leave, you should be thinking about succession plans. Even if you've failed to adequately plan for this eventual scenario, there are other really smart people, possibly already in your organization, who if given a chance can step up.

Everyone will hate me

If your team has an underperforming or misbehaving individual, the entire team already knows. Every other engineer on the team is quite aware of who pulls their own weight, who puts forth the extra effort, and who is a pleasure to work with. Dismissal of individuals with behavior that is misaligned to the culture is almost universally lauded by the remaining teammates.

The short of it is that moving fast to get someone out of your organization is almost always the correct thing to do for the company as well as for the individual. Leaving underperformers or badly behaving individuals on a team is affecting the entire team, adding unnecessary stress, and likely not mitigating any real risks.

The First Two Questions to Ask When Your Team Is Struggling

Cate Huston

I've never stepped into a leadership role without it quickly becoming clear why a new leader was needed. I think it's normal for companies to hire new leaders when there are problems that need to be addressed. So, I suspect that as the congratulations die down, it's also normal to look at the set of problems that surround you and ask, "Where do I begin?" (also normal: "What have I done?!"). I suggest, instead, starting with these two questions:

- How do I create *clarity*?
- How do I create *capacity*?

How Do I Create Clarity?

Every struggling team I have encountered seems to be experiencing some kind of existential crisis about "who we are" or "what is our purpose." Often this crisis is framed as a need for defining a "vision," but as a pragmatist (and someone who frankly hates the word "vision"), this seems beside the point. If we're not shipping, how much does it matter *what* we're not shipping? How can we possibly know what we should be doing two or five years from now if we don't have a consistent idea of what we are doing *today*?

Here's the thing about the "vision" problem: it's a comfortable one. No one on the team feels threatened by it, because it's largely someone else's problem. Everyone can have an opinion about it, because it's abstract enough that most people won't have to do anything to shape or change it. Vision debates are the "bikeshedding" of team purpose and structure: They're the sideshow discussions people have in order to avoid confronting more pertinent problems.

Clarity is more difficult because it's more immediate and must be based on what's happening *today*—which means you need to confront what's *actually* happening today—there's no hiding behind "lack of vision." Are teams delivering? Are projects drifting on and on with no end in sight? Are we doing things because they are *interesting* or because they are *valuable*?

The more concrete we get, the more difficult it is to get everyone in agreement: A wide range of opinions can find shelter in a broad, fuzzy statement in a way that is not possible in a narrow and clear one. Clarity involves hard conversations, hard truths, and defining one, then two, and then three steps ahead. It is challenging work that looks small from the outside—a "no" here, a "no" there, a refinement of this and that. It's often stating what at least some people believed to be true, anyway, such as what isn't going well or what the next steps include.

And yet, it's the most effective way I've found to stop teams from *drifting* and get them to begin executing.

What actions you can take in order to achieve clarity depend on the team, but typically you might try these:

- Take stock of all ongoing projects as well as the purpose and timeline for each of those projects.
- Clearly define the scope of upcoming milestones in every current (and new) project.
- Articulate the current priorities of the team, the purposes of those priorities, and the rationale behind making them priorities.
- Determine timeframes that you can predict (e.g., we are focused on X through the end of Q4) and highlight parallel work that will determine what comes next.
- Make sure project status is visible and that teams have visibility into each other's work (e.g., standup meetings).

How Do I Create Capacity?

Struggling teams also commonly suffer from a sense of overload. Often this is very unevenly distributed across the team—some people are exceptionally relaxed, whereas others seem alarmingly overwhelmed.

If you view your team as a system (*https://oreil.ly/OQuX_*), you'll see where you have bottlenecks (*https://oreil.ly/3nIr_*) that, if cleared, would increase the overall capacity of the team.

Perhaps you have teams that are working on too many disparate things (this usually involves people working alone). How do you streamline, focus, and make progress?

Perhaps your incoming requests are out of control. How do you stop checking off requests one by one and take a more strategic approach instead? What kind of help do you need to do that?

Perhaps you need to realign people closer to the work that they *want* to do.

Perhaps you need to give some people clear feedback about where they're falling short, and if that doesn't work, start the process of letting them go.

Usually people outside the team (leadership, marketing, etc.) are talking about dates and delivery, but you need to get the team itself estimating its timelines and embracing Continuous Delivery.

If you manage managers, improving them as leaders will always create capacity on your team: Their teams will become better, and you can rely on them more and delegate more effectively. Sometimes, it feels like we don't have time to coach the people around us, but medium term—not even long term—we don't have time *not* to.

OK, Now What?

It's likely that asking these questions has given you a whole lot of work to do. As you are human and can do only so much at once, now comes the question, "What do I do first?"

Answering this question is a balance between impact and time. The highest impact things you can do will likely take longer, but there are usually several relatively impactful things that won't take too much time. If you're new, you'll also have to balance building trust and demonstrating impact. For example, clearly communicating big-picture information about what is going on to the team is a worthwhile exercise that often uncovers new information is usually relatively quick, and it creates shared understanding across the team of where projects are at.

However, these smaller time investments will not have any impact unless we also take on some bigger ones. For example, there is nothing more corrosive to overall output than when one or more teams has a lead who is struggling or just isn't a good fit. Addressing this kind of situation is never straightforward and never easy—the only thing worse and more difficult, ultimately, is letting it continue unaddressed.

Every situation is different, so my suggestion is to write down a list of ideas for each, talk them over with your boss, a trusted peer, or a coach, and then begin taking them on one or two at a time. Just remember the list isn't static: as teams evolve, the bottlenecks change, and you'll need to keep asking these questions, revisiting and adjusting as you go.

The Five Whys of Organizational Design

Kellan Elliott McCrea

Recently, I wrote about sizing engineering organizations (*https://kella nem.com/notes/on-team-size*) and how you can think about it as an exercise in managing concurrency. In understanding organization size, I talk about the mental exercise of thinking about how the number of concurrent work streams you're taking on as a team applies upward pressure on the needs of your organization (e.g., you need more managers, who need more directors, who need a more senior CTO, etc.) The inverse exercise is also useful.

As is so often the case with conversations about organizational design, the problem statement usually starts like this: "We need a new engineering leader. Should we hire a new vice president of engineering and move all our managers there (except, of course, for that one team)? Should we hire a CTO to own architectural conversations but maybe not have anyone report to them? Maybe this half of our team could report to the CPO?"

I spend a lot of time trying to convince teams that this is the wrong way to think about organizational design. You can't solve questions of organizational design by shuffling responsibilities around the board like so many chips on the roulette table (or memorably, once, like so many stacks of Starburst candy on the floor of the CEO's office). And you can't solve your team's problems by slicing more thinly the responsibilities at the top, no matter how often someone tells you the hoary distinction that the vice president of engineering is there to manage people and the CTO is there to make technical decisions (a distinction that is not only bad and wrong, but will eventually leave your company a pile of burning rubble). These are the wrong questions. So, what are the correct questions?

Get Curious

When faced with these problems, I find it useful to walk the stack down to the front line of work to understand what the pressures on this complex system are. Call it the "Five (possibly rhetorical) Whys of Organizational Design."

Q1: Why can't your CTO/vice president of engineering/head of engineering create the context where these problems are getting solved?
A: Well, they're just spread really thin.

Q2: So why aren't your directors helping take the load off?
A: Well, they're spread really thin as well (or we don't have them).

Q3: So why aren't your engineering managers taking load off the directors?
A: They're spread really thin as well; we just promoted one of them from being a senior engineer, etc.

Q4: So why aren't your tech leads taking load off your managers?
A: They're spread really thin (or we don't have them).

Q5: So why aren't your senior engineers taking load off your tech leads?

And by now we often get to the interesting actionable answers.

Some Common Discoveries Along the Way

Having walked the hierarchy of organizational dysfunction, we can now start prescribing slightly more tailored responses than the leadership equivalent of "turn it off, and turn it back on again." Thankfully, many organizations face similar challenges, and we can catalog a few of the most common.

- Your head of engineering doesn't have anyone to whom they can delegate organizational work ⇒ you need directors.
- Your directors are spending all their time managing and can't contribute to organizational capacity ⇒ you need managers.
- Your managers are spending all their time dealing with the fact that their team is composed of humans ⇒ they either need fewer direct reports or to be managing people in a less drama-inducing work place.
- Your managers are spending all their time tech leading ⇒ you need tech leads.
- Your managers are spending too much time reviewing PRs ⇒ stop being a control freak and trust your team. You're hiring smart people to make good decisions. If you can't trust them, that's a leadership failure.
- Your managers are spending too much time coding ⇒ you need more engineers or you need to do less.

- You don't have tech leads because every team is super small, maybe one engineer per team ⇒ you're doing too many things. Also, you like failing.

- Your tech leads spend all their time reviewing PRs ⇒ seriously, stop it.

- Your tech leads and/or senior engineers spend all their time coding ⇒ your definition of senior doesn't include leadership. You need to fix that. Likely as far back as your hiring process.

- Your senior engineers are busy working on less-important things ⇒ it's *possible* communication has broken down. Or maybe prioritization isn't as clear as you thought it was?

- Your senior engineers are spending all their time firefighting ⇒ likely you've created insufficient slack in the system to allow for training and tool building.

- Your senior engineers don't have anyone to mentor/train, they're discouraged by the constant firefighting, they've become cynical about your lack of ability to plan, and they'd like to wander off and just build something shiny to give their brain a rest ⇒ did you do that thing where you "hire only seniors," because that's what it sounds like. Alternatively, did you do that thing where you spent a lot of energy selling your "hard technical problems" during your interview loop, but having those problems was a bit…aspirational?

- Your CTO/vice president of engineering/head of engineering doesn't actually want to think about any of these problems. ⇒ are you sure? Have you asked them? If so, you're right, you need a new head of engineering.

Focus on Growth to Improve Employee Engagement

Amy Rich

Managers often miss one of their employees' core intrinsic motivators: clearly identifying their growth paths. Taking time to set bidirectional expectations in a professional development plan shows that you, as their manager, are invested in their success, resulting in better engagement and performance, greater job satisfaction, and retention. Within 30 days of a new person joining my team, we take at least an hour to go through a document that contains the questions we look at here in a moment, helping me understand what makes them tick and setting expectations about their growth path over the next year.

What Is a Professional Development Plan?

A professional development plan is more than a random document of vague skills that an employee might aspire to learn.

- It's a holistic plan that melds the desires and needs of both you and the company and increases your ability to perform in your current job and/or your potential to perform in future roles.

- It's not focused solely on technical skills or just about conferences and training.

- It's not just about promotions (not everyone wants to advance beyond their current level).

The questions that follow are meant to help you discover where you want to go over the next year (or longer!). What do you like or hate doing? What are you good at? How do you measure up to your job level, and where could you improve to meet or exceed expectations? We'll create a concrete action plan to help get you there.

What motivates you?/What are your values?

This helps identify the kinds of things that you want to focus on because they're important to you. This includes intrinsic motivators as well as specific work activities.

What demotivates you?/What don't you want to do?

This helps identify the kinds of things that you *don't* want to spend much time doing, because they make you unhappy. Again, include intrinsic demotivators as well as specific types of work tasks.

What are your strengths?

Be generous with yourself; tell me all of the awesome qualities you bring to work. Start by thinking of the things that you like (from above) that you're good at. Read this article (*https://oreil.ly/79dh1*) for ideas about "soft skills," and also include your technical and business skills.

What are your goals?

What are the results you want to see by this time next year? Are there specific technical or business skills that you want to learn? Do you want to be promoted? What specific impact do you want to have on your team or the business?

What's our concrete action plan for getting you there?

These are concrete specifics of how to reach those goals. They can include education/training opportunities, projects you're interested in leading or working on, relationships you want to build, etc. We'll also specify how I can help you achieve those things and hold you accountable.

We dig deep, using the Five Why's, to get a really clear picture of the person's motivators, demotivators, and goals. Knowing this information attunes me to the needs of each employee and allows me to be a better manager for them, specifically. When we talk about the strengths section, some people tend to focus on just one of technical, leadership, or business skills and need a push to think about how well rounded they are across multiple dimensions. Using all of this information and my knowledge about what the team needs to succeed over the next year, we build a concrete, living action plan with specific (often prioritized) tasks.

We check back on their progress every month, and if there are performance problems, the skills required by the company shift, or they decide to focus on something different, we add/modify/delete items from the plan. We also use progress notes as one part of a continuous feedback loop and roll them up to the person's six-month reviews. This, along with regular discussions about competencies as measured by our job ladder, ensures that the employee always knows where they stand, where they're going, and what skills to focus on to get there.

If you aren't already creating professional development plans with your employees, try starting here, and see whether their engagement improves.

Followership

Jason Wong

Everyone likes to talk about leadership—we are culturally conditioned to view success as a progression through leadership positions—but far less attention is paid to being a good follower. In fact, when most people think of themselves as followers, it's often accompanied with negative feelings, like being judged as meek or submissive. As if being a follower comes at the expense of being a leader. But in reality, every leader in an organization is following someone, and so it serves us well to remember to live up to those responsibilities.

Models of Followership

There are many models of followership out there that give us a handy way of understanding follower behaviors for our reports and for ourselves. One model I'm fond of is the *Chaleff* model, shown in Figure 30-1, which describes two axes: the degree of support a follower gives a leader and the degree to which the follower is willing to question or challenge the leader's behavior or policies. These axes give rise to four distinct follower styles:

Resources display low support and low challenge. They do what is requested of them, but little more. They're just trying to get by and do just enough to retain their position.

Implementers demonstrate high support but low challenge. They take orders and don't ask questions. It's easy to love this type of follower because they just get things done. The downside is that they won't speak up when they see that the direction is not aligned with the company's ideals or vision.

Individualists demonstrate low support and high challenge. They tend to think for themselves and prefer to do as they want. This type of follower has no problem speaking up, but is often marginalized due to being consistently difficult.

Partners display both high support and high challenge. They are strong supporters but will provide challenge where they deem necessary. These types of followers are not afraid to speak up when something doesn't mesh with the best interests of the organization, but commit wholeheartedly to the corporate vision and the initiatives of the leader after a direction is decided.

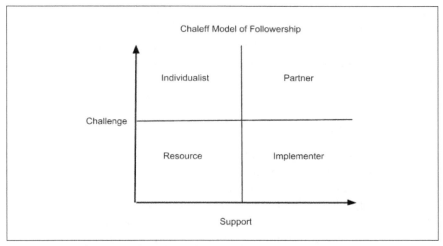

Figure 30-1. The Chaleff model of followership

Practical Application

To date, I've used this model in a number of ways. The first being, at a basic level, just helping me understand the types of folks in my organization and how to bring them together into productive teams. Identifying potential tech leads (partners) with a supporting cast and being cognizant of the difficulties that might occur if an individualist gets that role.

I've also used followership concepts to frame career paths by setting expectations around follower behaviors at every level on the career ladder. Starting engineers aren't expected to be implementers or partners. Software engineers, however, should be strong implementers, and senior software engineers and above should be developing their ability to be partners. With those expectations set, I can ask interesting career progression questions. Followership gives me a framework to direct my feedback. For example, Engineer A needs to grow from a resource into an implementer. Or, Engineer B is too much of an individualist, and I need them to be a partner.

In a day-to-day leadership role, I use followership to keep me honest about embracing and rewarding strong partners. When words are spoken that I'd prefer not to hear, understanding followership helps me remember the positives of being challenged, and I would be well served to consider what is being said rather than dismiss it out of hand. It helps me to avoid labeling people as troublemakers when they might, in fact, be influencing me in a better direction.

And, finally, I've used followership to evaluate how I am following my manager. How am I living up to my responsibility to stand up when I feel strongly about something in the company's interest? When my manager makes a decision, how am I undercutting or supporting them? What kind of follower does my manager need right now? These questions help me understand my performance and how I'm showing up in my role.

Conclusion

Good followers can influence leaders in positive ways that don't always come in pleasant packages. Some of the most impactful work I've done has come as a result of listening to folks who disagreed with me. Having a richer model for followership has helped me in numerous ways. As a follower, it helps clarify my responsibility to speak out and show support when appropriate. As a leader, followership reminds me that when I hear disagreement, it's an opportunity to take a beat, listen, and appreciate.

Forecasting with Less Effort and More Accuracy

Matthew Philip

When we estimate something, whether it's a batch of work or any particular single piece, the typical goal is to answer the question "When will it be done?" But do our traditional ways of estimating how long it takes to complete a task work? When we ask a group or individual to estimate *knowledge work*—work that by its nature is complex and unique—the information about the work is very low. Although more modern, Agile estimating practices (when done correctly) mitigate some of the pain of estimating—planning poker, for instance, is intended to reduce biases and time spent—estimating still requires time that we could spend on creating the software (opportunity cost) and involves multiple human biases. And we're still considering (and guessing at!) only a part of what accounts for delivery time: effort, or essential complication; that is, the amount of time it takes to do the job itself. Developers hate estimating, and managers hate nagging developers and missing deadlines.

Fortunately, we have *probabilistic forecasting*. A probabilistic forecast is simply a forecast communicated as a *range and a probability*. For example, most weather forecasts indicate the likelihood of some event occurring, such as snowfall:

- No accumulation: 11%
- Up to an inch: 48%
- One to three inches: 34%
- More than three inches: 7%

This is an appropriate and more realistic way of answering the "when" question because of what I call *Vacanti's Verity*: "When making a forecast (predicting the future), you must accept that there is more than one possible outcome."

Unless your team is doing CRUD (Create, Read, Update, and Delete) work in the same system for the 100th time, the delivery time is unknown. However, unknown doesn't mean *unpredictable*. Just how predictable your delivery system is will be conveyed in the probabilistic forecast, for which we'll use actual delivery data. Because we're concerned with determining delivery time (elapsed time between start and finish) of work, we'll collect start and end dates for our work items. You can track additional data such as work type, but to create our forecast, the pairs of dates are sufficient. We use these dates because within them are all the factors that affect delivery time and not only effort: blockers, rework, and work in progress to name a few. And it's because of these other system factors (which represent up to 85% or more of the total elapsed time) that our work items need not be the same size in order to forecast.

When we think probabilistically, we have real power—real as in the real thing, and not guesswork!—with which to plan and communicate with customers and others. Not only do we spend no time estimating, we can provide our customers with objective likely outcomes with which to make economic decisions. We know at any given time the answer to the question "When will it be done?" by running a *Monte Carlo simulation* of future outcomes.

This simulation (available in open source and pay options) basically uses our delivery-time data to generate all of those possible scenarios, from best to worst case and everything in between.

The result of a Monte Carlo simulation is a range of outcomes, with a percentage confidence at each. This allows us planning flexibility based on risk tolerance: for a very conservative, risk-averse need, we would use the 95th percentile, which tells us that 95% of the time, we expect to complete the given work, say, 42 work items in 25 days or less. If we're waiting to launch a marketing campaign, we might choose this confidence interval (or perhaps 85th). But if we're heading toward a fixed-date event with high reward potential—for instance, Apple's next announcement of a new watch—it might be worth it to "roll the dice" at the 75th or even 50th percentile. Planning now becomes a business decision based on risk. Also, it reduces stress and harmful pressures that influence the delivery team to (consciously or unconsciously) estimate in ways that can negatively affect their behavior and/or a trustful relationship with the customer. Further, it helps avoid the problem of estimates tending to lock us into initial solutions and bias us against discarding them in favor of better ones.

Answering the question for any particular piece of work is similarly simple. We just use our data to find our confidence intervals; for instance, we can graphically display this using a scatterplot chart showing delivery times for individual work items over time. We then look at our confidence intervals, drawn at the points where 95% of our items are below the line, 85% of them, and so on, and make the confident claim that "any next item is 85% likely to finish in 15 days or less."

The Four Layers of Communication in a Functional Team

Cate Huston

Functional teams have four layers of communication:

- A mission (also known as a vision)
- Strategy (made up of proximate objectives)
- Tactics and process
- Execution

This list might seem like it includes categories of action—it does. But it's not just *doing* these things, it's also *communicating* them that ties teams together. Communicating the items on this list plays a major role in scaling teams and leaders. With these things in place and communicated, it's much easier to add people to a team, and then entire teams to an organization.

The Mission

Personally, I hate the word "vision" because it has undertones of delusion, so let's use the word "mission" instead. An effective team has a mission around which they can rally. It provides a guide for what to take on—and what not to. On my own team, the goal is giving my company's mobile-only and mobile-first users a *great* experience. Having this mission gives us something to aim for and a sense of which feedback is important. It also connects us to our company's broader mission to "democratize publishing."

If the mission is missing, the team risks falling into an analysis paralysis or abdicating decisions entirely. Analysis paralysis can result from having no tiebreaker on decisions because data can be the only answer: there is no guiding principle, so it's easy for people to pick and choose the data to support their opinions. Abdicating decisions entirely can involve emphasizing the way the work is done rather than the work itself—either drowning in process or emphasizing a "culture" that is by its nature unsustainable, because it's not in service of anything else.

The Strategy

It's not enough to have a mission: We need to have a strategy that pushes us toward that mission. Strategies are *proximate objectives* (*http://goodbadstrat egy.com/about-the-book/*) that support the mission. For example, we might want to "deliver a sign-up flow that allows people to create a mobile-optimized website from their mobile devices" or "improve the media experience, resulting in more people uploading more media." These strategic objectives can be owned by subteams.

If the strategy is missing (or lacking), the case can be made that almost anything supports the mission, which can overwhelm a team and create indecision and conflict. Having an explicit strategy allows you to decide how the team you have can best move toward the mission.

The Tactics and Process

Tactics and process turn strategy into something that individuals can deliver on. They break down how work and communication are managed across teams. Adding this layer without having a strategy risks an elaborate performance of process (*https://oreil.ly/PvESQ*) in which most people will not see the value. This layer must support, not overpower, the strategy.

If both strategy and tactics are missing, it might be tempting to start with tactics, but you can't go too far if the aforementioned strategy layer is missing. On my team, this involves things like how we define features, how we measure performance of new features, how we make architectural decisions, and how we plan out and report on the roadmap within the theme of work the strategy lays out.

If tactics and process are missing, there is a huge overhead to any kind of coordination, and status is challenging to find (and maintain). No one knows what is going on and whether they feel like it's "good" rests entirely on emotion—the most inconsistent and challenging to measure of "metrics."

The Execution

The perfect mission-aligned strategy, even perfectly managed, still needs to be executed. This involves day-to-day communication around day-to-day work. It includes things like standup meetings and the way new task requests are made, reviewed, and merged. Having a lot of execution without the other pieces results in a lot of churn and detail-level activity that doesn't roll up into a coherent whole.

When execution is missing, it's obvious because very little happens. Projects might be well defined and communicated, but they don't move. The strategy might be clear, but no progress is made toward it. Everyone might buy into the mission, but it doesn't really matter when so little is getting done.

Other Ways to Define Team Communication

You can think of the four levels of communication as follows:

- Execution: how individuals work
- Tactics: how teams work and what enables them to work *together*
- Strategy: how a part of the organization delivers
- Mission: what the entire organization is setting out to do

Or:

- Execution: today/this week
- Tactics: this month/this quarter
- Strategy: next quarter/this year
- Mission: indefinite

These levels build on one another in both directions—the goal is not top-down or bottom-up, it's *balance*. Functional teams have harmony between all of these things. Dysfunctional teams have confusion at one or more levels. The irony, in my experience, is that often the concepts are there, but the consistent communication—the tying them together—is not. It's that absence of clarity (*https://oreil.ly/a37AS*) that is allowing disconnects and disillusionment to grow and grow.

The Four-Letter Word That Makes My Blood Boil

Marcus Blankenship

"JUST"

It's one of the worst four-letter words I know. Whenever I catch myself using it, I stop and apologize. And when I hear it, I hold up my hand and stop the person speaking.

Let me give you some examples from last week:

> "Just put a form up to collect their email…"
>
> "Just make it so they can log in with Facebook…"
>
> "I'll just throw it in a new database field."
>
> "We can just launch a new database server…"
>
> "Let's just let them post notes, like Twitter does…"

A synonym I often hear is "simply":

> "Let's simply use Redis for this…"
>
> "We'll simply spin up another AWS server…"
>
> "It should be simple to reuse the Atlas library for that."

If you use the words "just" or "simply," you might have forgotten how difficult the technical details can be.

Or, you might be pushing the team too hard and glossing over the details.

What If You're Not Saying It, But You're Hearing It?

Then it's time to stop the conversation and politely ask for the missing details. This used to be difficult for me because it made me feel like I was asking "stupid" questions. For many years, I felt that if I asked people to explain what they meant, I'd look dumb or unprofessional. Or I'd be wasting their time.

I finally realized that professionals aren't content with generalities or vague requirements. They stop and ask for specifics, even at the risk of looking dumb. They have the confidence to know they aren't dumb and to not pretend to understand something they don't.

You can use phrases like these:

"Let's pause so I can clarify what you mean. Are you suggesting that we…"

"Wait, before we continue, can you explain that feature more?"

"Going back to what you said, can you explain how you would implement that?"

"I might be a bit slow here, but can you explain?"

Lullaby Language

Jerry Weinberg calls "just" an example of *lullaby language (https://oreil.ly/ c9xfd)*, which "lulls your mind into a false sense of security, yet remains ambiguous enough to allow for the opposite interpretation." He groups it with words like "should," "soon," "very," and "trivial." All perfectly nice words that we see every day, but words that can carry a lot of hidden ambiguity and assumptions.

How I Learned to Stop the Conversation

My boss, Milind, was great at this. When I was promoted to team lead, I was brought into a whole new world of meetings and discussions, and I would keep my mouth shut when someone used the word "just" or spoke in vague terms. I didn't want someone to think I wasn't fit for the job or that I was having trouble keeping up. Instead, I nodded and smiled and tried to look like I was tracking with them.

But Milind knew it was dangerous to accept generalities or misunderstandings. He would stop a large group conversation with the phrase, "Maybe I'm missing something here, but can you explain that in more detail?" Everyone would look at him, the speaker would pause and then back up to cover the "just" part in more detail.

And, lo and behold, 90% of the time it was revealed that the person who glossed over the details had oversimplified something important. Or was wrong about an assumption. That means 90% of the time we were able to correct the discussion in the moment and move forward with better information.

And the 10% of the time there wasn't a problem? The explanation clarified everyone's understanding, and we quickly moved forward. Or it opened the door to other unspoken questions from the group.

Watching Milind do this made me feel confident enough to try it. Now I do it often because really understanding what someone is telling me is the most important thing. It allows me to correct misunderstandings and assumptions in the moment instead of wasting time working in the wrong direction.

Now It's Your Turn

How often do you hear the word "just" or "simply" and nod in agreement?

How could you pause the conversation and change it to move in a different direction?

How often do you use these words yourself, especially when setting expectations or defining requirements?

Friday Wins and a Case Study in Ritual Design

Kellan Elliott-McCrea

Culture is what you celebrate. Rituals are the tools you use to shape culture.

Yet very few of us think much about ritual design.

A standard piece of software development practice that many teams let lapse, or merely let lapse into being suboptimal is "Friday Wins," sometimes called sprint demos or sprint reviews. But you can take what can be a flaccid and repetitive meeting and make it a valuable ritual by grounding it in values.

When I'm designing Friday Wins, here are the handful of values I'm thinking about in my ritual design:

Learning oriented

Learning-oriented cultures look forward to and eagerly participate in reviews. If your team dreads postmortems or has lackluster end-of-sprint reviews, it's likely that you aren't facilitating a learning-oriented culture. Rather than saving reflections for when something has gone wrong, make the cadence of a weekly Commit-Reflect cycle the heart of your software process, and make reflection a thing to look forward to.

Call it "Friday Wins" versus "Sprint Review."

Organizational awareness

The insight that you can't predict who needs what information in a complex system drove NASA's original "systems management" insight, and most high-performing technology organizations since. (see also Team of Teams). Friday Wins should be maximizing for ambient awareness and chance encounters.

Don't silo wins by team. Invite the largest number of people who can reasonably attend. Invest in making attendance easy (support for remotes, no meeting policies, etc.).

Shipping

If you've worked on one of my teams, you know that I believe that a relentless focus on shipping is the primary driver of team effectiveness. Shorter cycle times have been shown to lead to both higher productivity and greater happiness. Value and learning are both primarily captured only after a project is finished. Confidence is gained most quickly in production. And so on, and so forth. If shipping is one of your values, center it in in your rituals.

Do not present work at wins that's almost done, almost done waiting for a PR, will be merged to master next, is merged to master but hasn't been deployed. Wins need to align with your values.

Modern software is cross-functional
Graphs count as wins, UIs count as wins, analysis of customer request behavior counts as a win, a new training module rolled out to the company counts as a win.

How software is made is important (part 1)
Most modern companies can succeed only when there is a high degree of mutual respect between different disciplines within the company.

One small part of that is Friday Wins that include people who aren't on the software engineering team (this is a value that is distinct and in addition to Organizational Awareness).

How software is made is important (part 2)
In a "tech company" or "tech-led company" the value and limitations of software is generally understood to some degree. As software continues to transform more problem areas it is important that the process of building software is understood and respected (in both its strength and limits). One key building block for this is making sure high-prestige individuals outside of engineering demonstrate that they care not only about results but about the process.

Invite the CEO to wins.

Inclusive and high energy
This is a weekly celebration. We have rules (time limits, only things in production, etc.), but it should be something people look forward to (or you should burn it down). This means that everyone should have a way to participate, even if you didn't have a "win" this week, and that everyone should be expected to participate, and that as a leader you need to make that a thing people look forward to.

Have an alternative method for playing; for example, show a win or answer a weekly "icebreaker"-like question.

Be prepared to draw folks out who don't recognize their own wins, and occasionally be prepared to put the win in the larger context of the goals.

These are the things that *I* think about when I'm designing an end-of-week ritual. A lot of these values will bubble up in other rituals I design because they reflect culture values I want to see on my teams.

The point isn't that this is how you should design your sprint reviews or "Friday Wins." The point is to be intentional in how you design your rituals.

Get Deployment Right on Day One

James Turnbull

Deployment gets the code you and your team have written out into the world. Any system you've written that isn't deployed and in front of a user isn't generating value. It's also not giving you feedback about your product and how it helps your users. Hence, getting deployment going is one of the first things most engineering teams (even if that's just you on day one!) do when they begin to build a product.

Like most items constructed at the start of a company or product's life, we often create the fastest, simplest *solution* hack as our deployment system: "I just need something that works, and I'll worry about making it better later."

This is a mistake.

The system that gets your code from your engineers to the customer is the most crucial piece of engineering tooling you'll build—*ever*.

The capabilities, quality, and performance of your deployment system directly correlate to the speed to market of your product, both in generating value and addressing user feedback and issues. Not only this, your deployment frequency and outcomes represent one of the (rare) early measurements of engineering velocity and quality. If your product or business partners are complaining about things moving too slow, this is one of the first places you should look. Finally, getting code in front of users and seeing your product in action makes your engineers happy.

You might get a lot of pressure to develop features and not spend time on this kind of tooling, as a manager you need to make sure that you have given the team room to develop this tooling.

Building That Deployment System

When you build that crucial first deployment system, you need to build upon the appropriate principles: what can be summarized as "CI/CD," or Continuous Integration/Continuous Delivery:

- Everybody should be able to deploy.
- Deployment should be automatic and continuous.

You can then scale your deployment system instead of refactoring it every time your organization scales. This comes with some risk of premature optimization but I believe that risk is outweighed by the rewards: faster deployment, enhanced developer happiness, and faster speed to market.

Let's look at each principle.

Everyone Should Be Able to Deploy

Everyone on your team should be able to deploy (Figure 35-1). A good deployment system should be continuous and not gated. Deployment systems triggered by intermediaries, "approvers," or small groups, like QA teams, are inherently hamstrung. First, this model removes a developer's ownership of the deployment of their code and its outcomes. Worse, it sometimes transfers ownership of the code that is being deployed, disconnecting an engineer from the reality of the systems for which they write code. Second, these models are slow by design. They exist to put roadblocks in the way of your code being deployed.

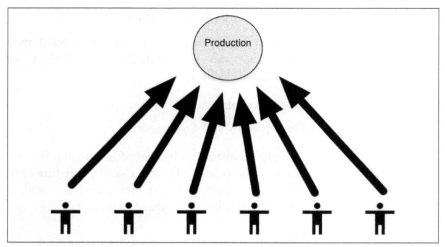

Figure 35-1. Every team member must have the ability to deploy

Deployment Should Be Automatic and Continuous

Code sitting in repositories or in branches is also not adding value. Any deployment process should optimize for putting the system into use as fast as possible. My preference has always been to automatically deploy to production any code merged to "master," as demonstrated in Figure 35-2.

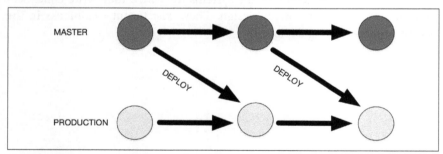

Figure 35-2. Automatically deploying from "master" to production

There has also always been a lot of debate[1,2,3,4,5] over how to manage development and code branching processes to get that code merged. Again, my personal preference has always been to make use of GitHub flow (*https://oreil.ly/eASKX*), which states:

1. The "master" branch can always be deployed.
2. Everything is branched off "master" and named for a feature or issue.
3. Do your work on that branch locally and regularly push your work upstream to the server, as illustrated in Figure 35-3.
4. Merge by opening a pull request, having it reviewed, and then merging it to "master."
5. Automatically deploy "master."

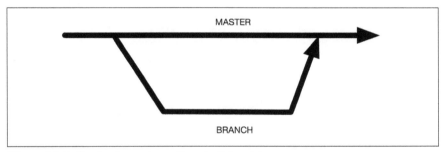

Figure 35-3. Deploying using a "master" branch

With the GitHub flow, we optimize for small, short-lived branches to reduce the risk of merge conflicts and disruption and to increase the velocity of code being pushed and deployed. Your commit-to-deploy time is another good, early measure of your team's development velocity.

If you are worried about interdependencies or features being developed over longer time frames—for example, in stages—you can make use of *feature flags (https://oreil.ly/cmoF-)* to hide features that aren't ready for prime time or not yet complete. Feature flags also encourage early user and integration testing. They additionally provide your engineers with a sense that a feature

1 *https://oreil.ly/DUW1a*
2 *https://oreil.ly/D09sv*
3 *https://oreil.ly/Ybkk9*
4 *https://oreil.ly/PkXI_*
5 *https://oreil.ly/L8NpA*

is evolving and work is progressing rather than being stuck in a long-lived branch.

If you do have to put in an approval process to satisfy compliance or regulatory requirements, the GitHub flow allows you to lock off the "master" branch from direct pushes and require approvals on pull requests.

Deployment FTW

After you have a deployment system that provides everyone on your team the ability to deploy automatically and continuously, the return on investment will be tangible and measurable. If your deployment system meets these two objectives, you're building on a good foundation that will allow you to scale as your team and company grow.

Good Process Is Evolved, Not Designed

Will Larson

Time management (*https://oreil.ly/bXXUM*) is an ongoing challenge for managers. Although there can be a certain heady rush to being relentlessly busy, I'm convinced that far more senior managers are overwhelmed with work than they want to be. What's a bit scary to contemplate is that they're overwhelmed by work generated from processes that they themselves were heavily involved in designing.

Process design (*https://oreil.ly/30dZj*) is a foundational skill for well-run organizations, yet is often treated as an afterthought. Individual processes garner a great deal of attention, but we rarely speak about how to create process effectively. The good news is that success here doesn't require innovation or novelty: adopt a structured approach and you'll quickly become an effective process designer.

How to Evolve Process

When we talk about creating a process, we almost always say that we *designed* a process. Design is a great word, because it implies the kind of careful thoughtfulness that great process does indeed possess. However, it's also a misleading word, because great process never emerges from the *Feynman algorithm* ("write down the problem, think very hard, write down the solution"), but instead derives from guided evolution.

Here's the algorithm that I've found effective:

1. Identify problem statement
There is a problem that either you have identified or folks you support have raised. Refine this into a problem statement that captures the problem you want to solve ("We want everyone to have the opportunity to apply to lead special projects.") along with the constraints you want to

respect while doing so ("We want to retain our ability to select project leads quickly.").

'2. Document approaches

It's easy to simply apply the approaches you're most familiar with; so easy, in fact, that it's the most prevalent failure mode of leaders who join a new company. Take some time to reach out to folks at other companies and learn how they approach the same problem.

3. Test approach

Identify a reasonable approach, not necessarily an amazing one, and give it a limited test run. The best test run is cheap and narrow (*https://oreil.ly/GDvhi*), optimizing for rapid feedback over a perfect approach. Trialing a process within a small team is surprisingly effective because it allows you to learn whether that process works before you begin advocating for wide adoption. Companies have limited bandwidth to adopt and maintain process, so it's helpful to weed out ineffective processes early. Small rollouts make it cheap to iterate and improve.

4. Iterate approach

With your updated problem statement, adapt or replace your approach with another reasonable idea. Then, return to testing it! It's generally the case that after you've identified the proper problem statement, the approach will be almost disappointingly simple. That's a good thing.

5. Practice

After you find an approach that works reasonably well, folks often want to begin evaluating it immediately, but that's often ineffective. The first time an organization uses a new process almost never goes super well; it takes time to learn new things, particularly when you need hundreds of folks to change at the same time. Run practice sessions, publicly describe success stories, and ensure everyone builds experience using it.

So now we have an algorithm for designing process, but honestly you already knew this was the best way to design process. That's the most interesting discovery when chatting with folks about how to design process: they already know how.

Why, in that case, do we keep making ineffective processes?

Why Good People Make Bad Process

Almost every bad process I've encountered has had the same problem: the problem statement is wrong. At best this leads to inert processes that solve scenarios that don't exist; at worst they're overactive, causing great inconvenience while doing little good. A common example in Silicon Valley companies is wanting to manage operations teams with a "churn and burn" mentality, but also wanting to be a company that inspires loyalty and high retention. This can lead to statements emphasizing ongoing education and career mobility coupled with processes that hinder such development.

Designing great process requires honest alignment on goals, methodical approach, and a great deal of thoughtful attention. Without all three, you'll rarely enact great process, and in the rare case where you do, it will decay quickly across context changes.

That's the bad news, but the good news is that great process builds momentum for more great process. The time you spend evolving it will come back to you, which makes evolving good process the single highest leverage act of management.

A Good Standup

Camille Fournier

I'm a proponent of standup meetings. I think they're one of the best of the Agile rituals. They are designed to be brief and focused, to give everyone on the team a chance to talk, and to set a pattern of open communication.

And yet, many people hate standups. What's worse in my mind, people have replaced standups with Slack bots that do little more than ask everyone their status for the day. Given that most synchronous standup meetings seem to be about sharing status, why does a Slack bot that collects the same information feel so wrong to me?

One way to define a good standup is to go back to "capital-A" Agile principles. In this world, a good standup looks at cards or stories, determines what has been finished, updates progress on things that are in flight, and identifies anything that is blocked. My gut reaction is to hate this idea of a good standup. Dictating a lot of Agile ritual to follow feels like going in the wrong direction, at least from the perspective of teams who already question the value of standups. I want teams to embrace standups as a lightweight and low-process event. Moving around cards and talking about tickets feels like the opposite of that.

However, this does get to the heart of what a good standup is about. A good standup is a constant reevaluation and refocusing tool for the group. A good standup answers the following questions:

- Are we working on the right things?
- Are we making the kind of progress we expected to be making?
- Have we gathered new information in the course of the past day that should change what we're working on now?

Using cards or other more formal status tracking is one way to do this. I think that's a great thing when you're in the final dregs of a known project, trying to burn down the remaining items as quickly as possible. But when you're in a period of time when you don't have immediate urgency around a project, you might have several days go by when there is little obvious movement. And yet, it is important that you are checking in as a team and reevaluating what you are working on even, or perhaps especially, in those quiet times.

Why? Because experienced engineers know that one of the most difficult parts of writing software is that there are frequent unknowns. These unknowns can pop up at any time, but they are most common in the early and middle stages of a project. Early on, there might be an understanding that the timelines are fluid and urgency is not yet a factor. Delivering software with any sort of predictability requires us to react quickly when we discover that we've hit on these unknown challenges. We need to decide whether to continue on the current path and expect a longer timeline or look for a different approach. Maybe someone else on the team has an idea to quickly resolve the newly discovered issue. The information you get in a daily standup should help the team react to these unknowns and adjust plans accordingly.

As an engineering manager, you're going to lead all kinds of teams. You'll lead teams that live and die by formal Agile processes, teams that reject anything that seems at all like a process, and everything in between. It is your job to keep the team's eyes on the priorities with a process that works for them. You need to get them to regularly ask and answer those key questions:

- Are we working on the appropriate things?
- Are we making the kind of progress that we expected to be making?
- Have we gathered new information that should change what we're working on now?

A bot is unlikely to get this for you, but neither is a simple status meeting. So, if you decide that standups are the best thing for your team now, make sure they are driving focus and prioritization for the team. If nothing ever changes because of a standup, what is the point in doing them at all?

Ground Rules in Meetings

Lara Hogan

> *Research shows that all human groups use rules of engagement to make something that can be very unpredictable (humans and human conversations) be a little more predictable.*
> —Paloma Medina, Ground Rules 101 (https://oreil.ly/vIoQU)

When you're in a meeting with six or more people, you might find that the group dynamics become a little unstable. One person looks checked out: they're on their laptop, you can hear Slack dinging. The person dialed in over video has stopped asking, "Could you move closer to the microphone, please?" and has resigned themselves to not being able to participate in this meeting. Another person has now dominated the conversation, continuing to make the same point in new and different ways.

Ground rules are here to help. When I'm facilitating a meeting, I usually pick three to five ground rules to rally everyone around at the beginning, customizing them to the needs of the meeting (what's needed for us to make progress, or keep things on track, or collaborate effectively, etc.). As I learned from Medina, ground rules should be short and easy to remember, but avoid being overly cutesy or gimmicky. Use ground rules to keep the meeting on track toward its goal. Here are the common ways I use ground rules and some examples you can use right away!

- Attend on time, every time
- Optimize for deciding and acting

You can also use ground rules to help attendees self-manage their participation and attention, especially when you have remote participants:

No laptops/phones/smartwatch alerts
   Unless you're remote, in which case, please keep only this video window open.

Use hand signals to participate
> Point to the ceiling to add something new, point at the person who's currently speaking to add on to their point, and use "jazz hands" when you can't hear or something else has gone wrong.

And you may also have ground rules to help attendees feel safer as they share information:

Vegas rules
> What happens in this meeting, stays in this meeting.

Stay curious
> Use open questions. Listen to learn.

Ground rules are the foundation for all that comes afterward: they might inform who you invite to a meeting, shape resulting deliverables, and affect the ways in which you achieve the meeting's goal. For example, when I ran a working group for Meetup to help define the company's architecture principles, I wanted to emphasize that we were using a representative leadership model. I included these ground rules:

Optimize for deciding and acting
> This is one of Meetup's company values. Reinforcing it as a ground rule helped the group avoid a potential failure mode in which participants optimized for full consensus, which would have dragged out our process indefinitely.

You're representing a part of Meetup Engineering; speak for them, not just for you
> We weren't there to voice personal opinions; we were there to represent a subset of the organization.

Let's act transparently
> This was a cue for each representative to keep their subset of the organization informed of our working group's progress. Everything that happened in the room was fully shareable outside of it, too.

Remind participants of the ground rules at the top of every meeting so that they become baked in and won't slip over time. As the facilitator or meeting leader, curb behavior during the meeting that breaks a ground rule. It's okay if this is awkward—I promise, it becomes easier as the rules are enforced because the group begins to remember them more and help curb one another, too.

Apply ground rules today to help achieve your meeting goals fairly and effectively. Ground rules can of course change over time: new folks are introduced and meeting goals might shift to warrant new rules. As Medina says, spending a bit of time at the outset setting these rules of engagement "consistently sets a foundation for human-friendly communication and minimizes the need for mind reading."

Help Yourself to Better One-on-Ones

Vrashabh Irde

One-on-one meetings are a critical part of running healthy engineering teams. For engineering managers, they're the most important meetings of the week—uncancellable time slots dedicated to listening to engineers on their teams. Although there is a lot of literature (*https://oreil.ly/cADaE*) on the internet about how to run good one-on-ones for managers, there seems to be little emphasis on the fact that *one-on-one meetings are actually engineer driven*. The time set aside every week is your opportunity as an engineer to broach critical topics for conversation. Here are some tips on how you as an engineer can make these conversations valuable, help your manager better recognize their value, and help yourself to perform better.

Bring an Agenda

I cannot stress this enough. As with any meeting, it's important to come to a one-on-one with a preplanned agenda. A good way to do this is to maintain a shared Google Docs file with your manager and prepopulate it with the agenda that you want to address in the next meeting. As you go through your week, add to this file the things that you want to discuss so you don't need to scour for topics at the last minute. If it's still empty before your next one-on-one, maybe it's a great opportunity to talk about career progression, growth, and giving feedback to your manager. Which brings us to…

Talk About and Build Career Goals

One-on-one meetings are the *perfect* time to bring up any skills that you want to improve on, new things you want to learn about, or a new role that you aspire to grow into. Your manager likely already knows about various opportunities in the company of which you're not aware. Making your career and skills growth a regular part of your one-on-ones are more likely to pair you with any new career opportunities that might arise. It also creates an opportunity for you to document regular progress between review cycles and learn how to get to where you want to go. Harvard research says that best way to stay motivated at work (*https://oreil.ly/CBPDs*) is by achieving and documenting small wins, and one-on-ones are a great place to do that. However, although this is important, one-on-ones are a great place to just talk about how you feel.

Talk About How You Are Feeling

Tech companies and startups are a cauldron of difficult conversations, deadlines, stressful situations, and politics and can have a strong impact on the mental state of individuals. One-on-ones generally are misconstrued as a place for doing status updates. This is certainly not the norm, and I generally recommend for my engineers to open up about their mental state and how they are feeling about the work they are doing, the environment they're in and the future as they see it. As engineers, you have the freedom to pick up any discussion, put it on the agenda and talk about it during the meeting. The one-on-one is meant to be a safe space for discussions. These crucial conversations help your manager make recommendations and set you up for success in your career. It can also help your manager detect burn out and put plans in place to help you.

Agree on a Format

Although some one-on-ones can be just conversations without structure, I generally recommend agreeing on a format with your manager on how to structure them. I've seen success by structuring 20 minutes of every one-on-one conversation to focus on the agenda and the next 10 minutes focused on career conversations. Structure allows for conversations to be focused.

Hold Your Manager Accountable

It's important to follow up on actions and discussions that happen in one-on-ones. Engineering managers generally have a *lot* going on, so it's very useful if you as an engineer take the initiative to make sure actions are followed up on and the proper conversations are had. Capturing one-on-one conversations in a Google Docs file like I mentioned before is one way to make sure this happens, and it helps to hold your manager accountable if there are any follow-ups.

Give Feedback

One-on-ones are not a one-way street. When you show a little empathy and accommodation for your manager, it makes them more likely to want to do the same for you. A great way to do that is to provide feedback. It builds trust, which is an invaluable capital to have with your manager and management team. Effective one-on-one meetings are a two-way street. Take a few minutes to talk about ways you can help them, and you're more likely to get what you want, too.

Push Back Hard Against Cancellation/ Postponing

Good engineering managers will always prioritize one-on-one conversations over any other meetings in their calendar. Hold them to this and try to make it to every one-on-one that has been scheduled. If they need to cancel for any reason, it's ok to ask them why and make sure it gets rescheduled.

How Do Individual Contributors Get Stuck?

Camille Fournier

As a new manager, you will become responsible for providing feedback to the people on your team. If you aren't a naturally critical person but you want to give someone a valuable insight, you might find this task daunting. To that end, I suggest the following:

> Pay attention to how they get stuck.

Everyone has at least one area on which they tend to get stuck. An activity that serves as an attractive sidetrack. A task they will do anything to avoid. With a bit of observation, you can begin to see the places where your team members get stuck. This is a super power for many reasons, but at a baseline, it is great for when you need to write a review and want to provide useful constructive feedback.

How do people get sidetracked? How do people get stuck? The lists that follow (which are not comprehensive) can get you started.

Individual contributors often get sidetracked by:

- Brainstorming/architecture: "I must have thought through all edge cases of all parts of everything before I can begin this project."
- Researching possible solutions forever (often accompanied by desire to do a "bakeoff" where they build prototypes in different platforms/languages/etc.).
- Refactoring: "This code could be cleaner and everything would be just so much easier if we cleaned this up… and this up… and…"
- Helping other people instead of doing their assigned tasks.
- Jumping on fires even when not on-call.
- Working on side projects instead of the main project.

- Excessive testing (rare).
- Excessive automation (rare).

Individual contributors often get stuck when they need to:

- Finish the last 10–20% of a project.
- Start a project completely from scratch.
- Do project planning (You need me to write what now? A roadmap?).
- Work with unfamiliar code/libraries/systems.
- Work with other teams (please don't make me go sit with data engineering!!).
- Talk to other people (in engineering, or more commonly, outside of engineering).
- Ask for help (far beyond the point they realized they were stuck and needed help).
- Deal with surprises or unexpected setbacks.
- Navigate bureaucracy.
- Pull the trigger and going into prod.
- Deal with vendors/external partners.
- Say no, because they can't seem to just say no (instead of saying no they just go into avoidance mode, or worse, always say yes).

"AHA! Wait! Camille is missing something! People don't always get stuck!" This is true. Although almost everyone has some areas in which they find themselves overly hung up, some people also get sloppy instead of getting stuck. Sloppy looks like never getting sidetracked from the main project but never finishing anything completely, letting the finishing touches of the last project drop as you rush heedlessly into the next project.

Noticing how people get stuck is a super power, and one that great tech leads and managers rely on to get big things done. When you know how people get stuck, you can plan your projects to rely on people for their strengths and provide them help or even completely side-step their weaknesses. You know who is good to ask for which kinds of help, and who hates that particular challenge just as much as you do.

The secret is that all of us end up stuck and sidetracked sometimes. There's actually nothing particularly bad about this. Showing people how it happens allows them to decide how to address the issue. They can try to overcome the fears that are sticking them, such as lack of knowledge, skills, or confidence. They can consciously avoid such tasks as much as possible. And best of all, they are now aware of their habits and can use extra diligence when tackling these areas.

So, use these lists to pay attention and bring specifics the next time you need to give feedback. No one likes to feel stuck, and they'll be grateful you are there to help dig them out.

How to Be Discerning Without Being Invalidating

Akash Bhalla

First, some context:

I'm at my company's 2017 Christmas party. It's a relatively classy affair. We're on a boat cruising along the Thames while people mingle and talk, enjoying the faux casino that's been set up on board.

I'm at the bar chatting with Samantha, our head of people, and the conversation turns toward hiring. Sam asks if I'd had the opportunity to speak much with one of our newer hires. I tell her I haven't.

She tells me I should; we'd get on very well, she feels, particularly because of my personality — I'm "very cynical." I'm pretty sure it was meant as a compliment, akin to being realistic or discerning; however, it sticks with me and I can't help but return to the thought over the next few weeks.

I'm cynical.

Being Realistic

I'd like to think I'm realistic (or pessimistic?), not cynical.

In some ways, realism is a fundamental quality of good software engineers. A keen eye for detail and a methodical, logical approach to problems. Being able to connect to the reality of a situation and planning accordingly.

Although a more optimistic or hopeful person might see a feature or requirement and think of all the problems that it will solve, the eagle-eyed engineer will look at it and think of all the scenarios in which it will fail.

Both are essential, of course. You need hopeful optimism to build a vision of a better future, and you need grounded realism to achieve it.

When harnessed correctly, this "grounded realism" can be extremely powerful and useful. As a developer, it's a useful skill for focusing in on edge cases and "sad paths" when building a feature or analyzing a codebase or system. It also helps in accurately scoping a piece of work and building a reliable product.

The Danger of Being Too Realistic

This ability or quality of being realistic has its value when applied to a work context, as just mentioned. However, it's a slippery slope, and this mentality can easily lead to you becoming overly judgmental and critical of other people's choices. You begin to assume that your way of thinking is the only one of any value, and other approaches or styles are invalid.

I have found this a difficult transition as my role has changed. I spent a decade as a software developer and honed my ability to think in terms of code and logic, spotting edge cases in a world that is pretty black and white and failure is more binary. But I have now moved into a head-of-engineering role that is much more focused on people and management, where the scope goes beyond the system and code, and there are more shades of gray.

An immediate example comes to my mind. We run a regular book club at work themed around management and leadership; the current book we're all reading is *Legacy*, by James Kerr. I've never read it before, but some members of the team are big fans, and it is one of Sam's favorite books.

I strongly disliked the book, and it took considerable effort to get through it.

My first instinct was to be aggressively dismissive and critical of the book without regard for other people's opinion. It was only after being challenged that I realized what I was doing.

Yes, I disliked the book; it clearly wasn't something that I enjoyed or that resonated with me. Yet, it was equally clear that others had the complete opposite reaction to it; they found it inspiring and captivating.

There is nothing wrong with the book. There is nothing wrong with the people who liked it. There is nothing wrong with me. There is just a mismatch, and that's fine. The book isn't written for people like me, but that doesn't make it inherently bad. I need to learn to stop and think before rushing to criticize something and instead try to recognize and appreciate that I might just not be the intended audience.

It's the difference between:

"This is s---."

and:

"This isn't for me."

Adapting to a New Role

With this shift in my role, I'm learning that the most important thing for me is no longer being able to spot edge cases and failure scenarios from a hundred paces. There are far more skilled developers than me working here that can do that.

My focus now needs to be on creating a validating environment at work in order to nurture the people and the culture of the organization. I need to learn to maintain an ability to be discerning yet balance that with an ability to encourage and nurture.

Squashing bugs and inefficiencies when building a product is a skill to be proud of. Squashing ideas, dreams, and opinions is not.

How to Conduct an Autonomy-Support Meeting

Matthew Philip

The fifth principle of the Agile Manifesto encourages us to "Build projects around motivated individuals, give them the environment and support they need, and trust them to get the job done." As managers, one of the ways we can fulfill that principle is by providing *autonomy-support meetings* for the people we support.

An autonomy-support meeting is a one-on-one meeting in which the manager, taking a servant-leader stance, helps an employee by clearing a path and clarifying what problems need to be solved but not how to solve them.

Rather than telling the employee what to do, the manager asks what they can do to support the employee's goals in alignment with the team's and organization's goals. Here are some ways in which a manager can do this:

- Seeing issues from the employee's point of view
- Giving meaningful feedback
- Receiving feedback from the employee
- Providing choice over what to do and how to do it
- Encouraging the employees to take on new projects or roles
- Making clear the team and organizational goals

The dynamic should be one in which the traditional organizational structure is flipped upside-down. That is, rather than the traditional dynamic of the employee "working for" the manager, in the autonomy-support meeting, the servant-leader has the mindset of "working for" the employee. In this way, the manager typically doesn't give the employee to-do items but rather takes their own to-do list from the employee.

Autonomy-support meetings are an opportunity for the employee to give feedback on how their manager can help the employee realize career goals in the organization. The meeting can be scheduled by the employee or someone acting as the employee's advocate. Multiple managers might attend the meeting, depending on which ones the employee feels are vital and able to help.

As for topics, it's whatever the employee needs managers to do in order for the employee to do their job better or reach goals. This might be a request for a different project or role switch, more time to explore a particular skill or technology or simply clearer vision or expectations set. Premised on the manager's commitments to the employee, the employee has the right to ask the manager for support in various career-development goals, including timelines for when those things would occur.

Questions that you as a manager might want to ask:

- How can I help you realize your goals in the next year?
- By when would you like me to achieve these things for you?
- In what areas have I failed to help you in the past, and how can I improve?
- What kind of things would help you feel more engaged?
- How can I help smooth your path toward mastery of certain skills?
- What does success look like for you, and how can I help you succeed?

As a manager, I commit to you as an employee:

- Meet with you as often as you need (and at least semi-annually) to personally discuss how I can provide autonomy support, to the extent desired by you
- Help you prioritize your professional development and not merely view your employment as a matter of billability
- Be transparent about the organization's goals and work with you to align your goals with them to support your career progression within the organization

As Daniel Pink notes in his book *Drive*, "Researchers found greater job satisfaction among employees whose bosses offered 'autonomy support.'" If you're looking to help your employees find that greater satisfaction, flourish, and fulfill the promise of the Agile Manifesto, consider starting up autonomy-support meetings.

How to Help Your New Grad Engineer Navigate Work

Kaya Thomas

I started my first full-time job less than a month after I graduated from college. I moved across the country from the East Coast to the Bay Area, feeling ready to join the work world and be a "real" adult. Those first six months were a tough transition that no one prepared me for. Now, a couple of years later, I realized that many managers are often far removed from the transition that most new grads experience in starting their first job. I didn't know at the time how to communicate my struggles. In this essay, I go over conversations that you can have with your new grad engineer that can help ease their transition and teach them techniques to navigate the work world.

The new grad joining your team has just accomplished a big long-term goal: graduating college. With that under their belt, what's the next goal that they need to work toward? For some, that new goal might be to become a CTO, vice president, or principal architect, but what are the steps they need to take to get there?

While in school, the steps to graduation are clear: take a certain set of classes, pass them, and you get a diploma. In the work world, things aren't usually as explicit. As a manager you can have the conversation that helps your new grad set realistic short-term and long-term goals. Ask them what type of impact they would like to have in their career and translate those into goals. The most important step is to break those larger goals into mini-goals. Smaller and short-term goals are less overwhelming and can be just as rewarding when it's clear how they relate to the larger goals you've set.

One of the most difficult things for me to grasp during those first few months at work was that your efforts would not directly translate into acknowledgement or promotions. As a student, the amount of work you put in was directly rewarded through your grades and you were able to keep track of all that work with your transcripts. I soon realized that, at work, your manager would not always know everything that you're doing and what you've accomplished that day or week. My manager encouraged me to keep a personal record of all my accomplishments, big or small. Encourage your new grad engineer to have their own record of their work, which should include not only their technical successes, but also their achievements in collaboration and communication. Documenting their achievements will help them better be able to advocate for themselves rather than expecting someone to keep track of what they've done and advocate for them.

After discussing goal setting and self-advocacy with your new grad, you can connect those to two topics to go over promotions and career growth. No matter what kind of career ladder or promotion cycle your company has, you can break it down in a similar way as the goal setting conversation. Which of the goals they've already set match to how they can grow in their current role? Which accomplishments did they write down in their record that they can use to show they are performing at the next level? These questions are a great way to make career growth seem more approachable because it relates back to previous techniques you've gone over. It's difficult to jump from being a student with a clear goal and end date in mind, to a full-time professional with decades of work life ahead of them with unclear expectations. These conversations can make a big difference in easing the stress of the transition and help prepare them for having a clear path to achieve in their career.

How to Share Decisions for Strong Execution

Katie Womersley

There's a lot of great research on how to make good decisions, more decisions, and faster decisions. But as a manager, getting the decisions made (well, fast, and by the appropriate people) is just the first step. You also need to make sure that these decisions are acted upon. This means that they need to be clearly understood, shared with the proper people, and can be easily referenced.

Being intentional about sharing decisions increases the quality of your team's decision making and builds stronger alignment across your team. Clearly communicating decisions is vital for a team to execute those decisions, yet many leaders struggle to do this effectively. Following are four methods that you can consider to help you sharpen your communications with your team:

1. Clarify the decision

To make and communicate decisions effectively, you need a very clear statement of what the decision is. Don't skip this step!

If you've ever been in a meeting and thought, "Wait…what are we deciding?" everyone's time is getting wasted. These meetings are worse than pointless: you are running the risk of everyone walking away with a different takeaway, having heard whatever it was that they wanted to hear. After this type of meeting, each person is then also likely to walk away mistakenly thinking that everyone else also supports their (unique) interpretation of events. After all, everyone else was in the meeting, too!

Avoid calamitous misunderstandings by clarifying the decision. Shared context is difficult to build, so start off strong with an obvious, clear decision statement.

2. Share that the decision making is happening

For bigger decisions, it's helpful to share ahead what decision is being made. This can be lightweight and quick— a point on a meeting agenda (make sure to share your meeting notes) or a quick email.

Knowing ahead of time that a certain decision will be on the agenda helps people to arrive prepared and gather their thoughts. Advance notice also helps include those more thoughtful, deliberate teammates who prefer not to think on their feet. You'll get more varied perspectives and a better-quality decision.

3. Decide and share who the decision makers are

For a simple decision, it's helpful to identify who the decision maker is: the person who will make the decision (and be accountable to the outcomes). For a more complex decision, doing a RACI (*https://oreil.ly/ CBPDs*) (Responsible, Accountable, Consulted, Informed) responsibility assignment matrix works well.

The "responsible" person, or decision maker, should also be communicating the decision. If it's unclear who will make the decision, you can end up with a bystander effect in which everyone participates in the decision, but no one takes ownership of (1) ensuring a decision is reached and (2) communicating the decision.

Bonus points if this person isn't (always) the manager. Effectively delegating decision making is a necessary step for building a strong, autonomous, empowered team.

4. Document the decision

After your decision is made, in whatever format you're using (via a meeting or as a conclusion from some research), you need to ensure two things: your decision is *communicated*, and there's a *record* of that decision that can be accessed later.

To share the content of a decision, *choose a communication method that's lower volume and more persistent.* For example, email works better than throwing a key decision into a fast-moving group chat channel. Having a document like a Google Docs or Dropbox Paper to record what the decision is and who the decision makers were is helpful to reference later on, too.

The decision should be shared to the widest group of people whom it might affect. A decision that directly affects product engineers but could be of interest to engineers outside product engineering (e.g., a DevOps team) might be shared to all engineers.

For bigger decisions, by the time you're at this stage, people should not be hearing about the decision out of the blue. They should have already heard that the decision is being made, why, and by whom. They might have even seen that decision be made in a meeting or followed along in your document. This is important so that by the time the decision is shared in a follow-up communication, it's much easier to process and retain. *Don't surprise people.*

Finally, you need to record the decision. Do any documents or workflows need to change? If so, update them promptly. Will this affect how teams work going forward? If yes, you'll need to update your team handbook/wiki. Do you just need a record that is a bit more accessible than email? It's handy to share your Dropbox Paper/Google Drive doc, put it in an appropriate folder, and link to that in a team "what happened this week" roundup. If you're not doing these things and you sense that your team could be more on the same page, this might be what's missing.

But This All Takes So...Tediously...Long

Yes, it does. But it's tremendously less time and effort than your team not know what's going on. Constantly putting out fires, redoing work, and repairing relationships because people weren't on the same page is far more time consuming than communicating intentionally. A team that all rows in the same direction gets there faster.

Improve Your Decision Making with Mental Models

Mathias Meyer

Whether you're a new or experienced engineering manager, the chances are high that you'll be finding yourself in similar situations all the time. Someone might repeatedly come to you with the same question, or you're observing the same kind of situation play out many times over.

Maybe conflict keeps bubbling up during a meeting. Or people fight over a specific tooling or approach for building a new feature. Or your engineers argue constantly about how important it is to fix an architectural problem over upcoming product priorities.

It's only natural to take each of these situations and respond as you see fit every time. Some of them might be influenced by how you're feeling at that moment, others by how close you are with the person who comes to you with a problem or question. As either varies throughout the day, it's likely that you'll end up telling different people different things, which will confuse matters more.

In these situations, it helps to build up a set of mental models, decision-making models, or frameworks. They're a set of responses that you go through when you're faced with certain situations. They allow you to move past an initial response, which tends to be driven more by emotions and intuition (which isn't a bad thing, we're all human after all), and move toward a more objective and structured response.

A simple example is one of your engineers coming to you to complain about someone not pulling their weight or not committing code frequently enough, or not living up to their commitments.

This engineer will tell you their story, and it's your job to dig deeper. Your first response could be, "What are they really telling me?" or, "What's really going on here?"

These two simple questions allow you to move past an initial urge to respond and think about the problem in front of you. They might not give you the answer immediately, but they provide pointers on where to go next. And that's what I've found to be key for effective decision models. They need to be concise and actionable, always giving you the next step.

One of my engineering leads comes to me with a question. I first ask myself "Should this person be able to find an answer on their own?" If so, I come back with "What do you think we should do?"

Maybe it's a question that this person currently isn't equipped to answer on their own; maybe because it's an organizational question. Then I go through these questions:

- Why did this person come to me with this problem?
- Am I the right person to solve their problem?
- If not, who is?
- Is this a unique occurrence, or is there a possibility for a precedent?
- If it is a precedent, what needs to happen to make sure that it's addressed now and for the future? Is there a process missing, or documentation? Or is a responsibility not fully clear?
- If I've deferred this person to someone else, when do I need to follow up to make sure they got their answer?

Or, take Eisenhower's decision matrix regarding when work should be done. It's a classic example of a decision-making model, and one I also like to have in my toolkit. If something is urgent and important, do it. If it's important but not urgent, plan on doing it soon. If it's neither urgent nor important, drop it. If it's urgent but not important, delegate it.

How can you build your own frameworks? You can begin by observing how you usually respond in situations similar to the one I just described. After the situation was resolved, articulate how you approached resolving the issue. Think about what kinds of questions and decision trees would bring you closer to a resolution and then write them down.

It's important to keep these frameworks light and simple. You want to be able to run through them quickly.

Or ask a more experienced manager to articulate theirs, by asking them how they would respond to a certain problem or scenario. These folks have mental models, whether they're aware of it or not. Sometimes it just needs someone (you!) to encourage articulating them.

Try them out when the next opportunity arises, and see whether the result is the one you'd expected. Refine and try again.

Over time, you'll build a kit of these models and frameworks, and they'll help you be fair, consistent, and clear with your team.

All three of them are, in my definition, key qualities of being a good manager.

Interviewing Engineers: Going Beyond Technical Skills

Alicia Liu

As an engineering manager, one of your key responsibilities is deciding who to hire into your organization. Engineering interviews tend to focus heavily on technical assessment, but for you to build an effective team, *soft skills* are equally important to evaluate. So-called soft skills are not soft at all; they're fundamental to teamwork. It doesn't matter how well an engineer can code if their code is unusable because they've neglected to communicate with coworkers. At worst, their behavior causes others to avoid working with them or even to leave your team. Every new team member changes the team dynamics, and you want to ensure that change is for the better.

First, decide what key attributes you're looking for in candidates. Communication skills are critical to assess, of course, but so are other skills key to collaboration and teamwork: being able to take and give feedback, to adapt, to effectively disagree, to self-reflect and admit mistakes. You might also want engineers who are great at mentoring, leading projects, or negotiating with external stakeholders. Discuss and articulate the nontechnical skills and attributes that are important to your team, that reflect your team's values, and that would strengthen your team.

After your team has agreed on what you're looking for, form a shared understanding of how to look for and evaluate candidates on these attributes. Making an effort to create a consistent interview process helps reduce bias. Without a shared evaluation framework, interviewers are prone to base decisions on unconscious biases, such as how similar the candidate is to themselves, or how likeable they find the candidate. You can compare candidates more equitably by asking them the same interview questions, and creating a rubric to guide interviewers on how to evaluate candidates' answers.

Don't just look for soft skills in the behavioral interview. Technical interviews are also great opportunities to evaluate a candidate on nontechnical attributes. The more you can make your technical interviews a collaboration between the interviewers and the candidate, the more signal you can get on how well this candidate will work with other team members. Having the interviewer collaborate with the candidate in a technical interview not only simulates a more realistic scenario of what it's like to work together, the candidate will also have a better experience than being grilled in an interview that resembles a computer science exam.

Involve a wide range of team members in the interview process rather than relying on only senior engineers as interviewers. You can uncover behavioral issues that might otherwise go unnoticed by adding an entry-level engineer as a second interviewer, or having a product manager or designer participate in collaborative software design interviews. This way, you can discover problems such as a candidate who is dismissive or condescending toward people they perceive to be less technical.

After the interview, when you are scoring a candidate across the range of attributes, treat technical skills differently from behavioral attributes. With technical skills, if a candidate is otherwise experienced but weaker in one area, it's not a deal breaker if there is room for them to learn on the job. Unlike accruing more technical knowledge, behavioral traits are difficult to change even when there is a willingness to change. As their potential future manager, consider any flags in these areas as serious deal breakers, even if only one interviewer reported it. By looking at scores on behavioral attributes separately, you avoid masking a candidate's lack of core soft skills with high technical proficiency.

Ultimately, you're not just hiring individuals, but members of a team. The overall output of your team matters more than an engineer's individual productivity. Likewise, your interview process should filter for the people who will improve your team overall, which encompasses a much wider range of abilities than technical skills alone.

Introduce an Engineering Ladder

Lisa van Gelder

You know you want to implement an engineering ladder at your company. What's next? If you just tell your engineers that you have defined a ladder and it now applies to them, you might find that they revolt!

As vice president of engineering, I've introduced an engineering ladder at two companies: Stride Consulting and Bauer Xcel. Here, I present the seven steps that I've gone through to ensure it has been successfully adopted.

1. Communicate the Why

You want your team to feel the ladder is for them. If your company has never had an engineering ladder, you need to be very clear about why you think now is the right time to introduce one and what problems you think it will solve. Explain how they will benefit.

2. Get Your Team to Define the Levels Themselves

You want your team to feel that the ladder is for them rather than imposed on them. The best way to do that is to task the team to define the ladder itself. I start by taking Rent the Runway's engineering ladder (*https://oreil.ly/ruZm0*) and adapting it to the organization. Then, I share it with the entire engineering team, along with some other example ladders (Kickstarter (*https://oreil.ly/jXpmW*), Meetup (*https://oreil.ly/1kJ-r*), Intent Media (*https://oreil.ly/xEib1*), etc.) and make the ladder editable by the entire company. Everyone gets a chance to add comments and define levels—including their own level—before the ladder goes into effect.

At Stride, I had a series of meetings with the seniors during which we went through each level, skill by skill, and agreed on definitions. At Bauer Xcel, I put stories into the sprint for every team to make sure people had time marked out when they could review the ladder and comment. Then, we created a Slack channel for people to discuss wording they disagreed with and come to a consensus.

3. Communicate the How—How Will It Be Implemented?

The team needs to understand what is going to happen once you put this ladder in place.

- What happens if people aren't acting at their current level? Are they demoted? Is there a grace period?

- What happens if a role people are performing is redefined? What happens if they feel they can no longer perform that role?

- What happens if people are acting at the next level up? Are they promoted? How much of the next level must people do before they are promoted?

- How is salary affected?

- How will this tie into the performance review/promotion process?

You'll want to think through all of the implications before introducing the ladder to your team. At Bauer Xcel, we sent out an anonymous survey asking about team preferences for how to handle level setting.

4. Try It Out!

Use your new engineering ladder in the performance review process and give folks the chance to discuss where they are on the ladder. I wouldn't use it for a formal performance review before people have had time to kick the tires a little, so I'd suggest doing a trial run on volunteers before using it for real.

How long does this take? In my experience it takes at least a quarter to roll out an engineering ladder. It takes time to go through the initial comments and create the levels, and then if you do a trial run as part of the standard performance review process, you might need to wait until the next performance review starts (at Stride, they were every six months) That's fine, it gives your engineers more time to get used to the idea. Hopefully, your volunteers are enthusiastic about how much the ladder helped them so that others are excited to use it next time!

---

5. Review

Gather feedback from your volunteers. Were some areas unclear? Were some skills missing from different roles? Give people a chance to adapt the ladder based on the review they just did. Open a final review round from the rest of your engineers, too.

6. Use for Real

Build the engineering ladder into the performance review process. After receiving feedback, engineers discuss where they are on the ladder with their manager and what they need to work on to get to the next level.

7. Make It a Living, Breathing Document

Skills and roles are constantly changing, and the ladder needs to adapt with them. I allow the ladder to be edited by the entire company before every performance review cycle, lock it during the cycle, and then allow editing again afterward.

Leadership Is About Responsibility, Not Authority

Seth Dobbs

I am often asked questions along the lines of, "The development team has more experience than I do, how can I be an authority to them?" This describes a difficult situation in which someone with less experience than the bulk of the team members has been promoted to a leadership role. A similar scenario is someone recently added to a team who has been working on a product for years and the newcomer architect has little depth of knowledge. In either scenario, the new leader needs to gain credibility in order to be effective or risk being undermined by the team. More broadly speaking, there can be a lot of discomfort in being a newly minted leader trying to tell a team what to do.

And that's exactly where the problem comes in: we as leaders shouldn't think our job is telling people what to do.

Thomas Chandler Haliburton, a nineteenth-century Nova Scotian politician and author, observed that, "Wherever there is authority, there is a natural inclination to disobedience." It sounds a bit like he's worked on one of today's software development teams! In fact, it can be fairly common among knowledge workers in general to question authority and to sound out the depth of a new leader's knowledge and then use their "superior" knowledge to discredit and/or disobey the leader.

So what's a new leader to do? For me, the answer forms one of my core principles of leadership:

> Leadership is responsibility, not authority.

In other words, we as leaders have a responsibility to make our team members succeed, not an authority to make our ideas hold.

This can be a difficult lesson. Some seek leadership roles because they believe it's about authority. And, sure, organizational authority is a thing. Authority can come with hierarchy and with depth of knowledge. Role power is real and can be used for good or ill. Indiscriminate use of authority and role power will often not yield durable results. Worse, it can't be used for situations in which you don't actually have hierarchical role power over the people you lead.

Looking back to the question that started this, the architect who first asked me this didn't have role power over the development team, which is often the case for leaders in flat organizations: the people they lead are matrixed in from other parts of the organization. The person also readily admitted to me that they had less experience and technical knowledge than the average team member.

So, the answer to the question, "How can I be an authority to them," is often, "You can't, but don't worry about that." Being a leader doesn't mean being the best "doer"; it means being a leader. So instead of trying to wield authority, I'd encourage you to tell the team that you're leading simply and directly that your responsibility is to help them succeed at their jobs. Get into a dialogue and find out what they need from you to succeed and help them help you by giving you what you need to succeed.

In the case of a new software architect, you're providing them guidance on how the broader system is coming together, and they in turn can provide you deeper details of what's been implemented A new development manager could let the team know you're there to help ensure the team delivers value to the business and that you need to understand constraints, risks, and trade-offs in time, budget, and scope so that you can manage expectations. An organizational leader should help the team understand that your responsibility is to help them grow in a meaningful way that ideally also benefits the company

It takes a little humility to approach leadership this way and perhaps even some rethinking of your role, but if you see leadership as a responsibility to help others succeed and take that responsibility seriously, you'll be one of the best leaders your team has ever had.

Leading Through Rapid Change Is Normal

Yvette Pasqua

Do you feel like you're constantly leading your team through one change after another? Have you wondered when it's going to end so that you can get back to your "normal" job of managing teams to ship software? Well, the truth is: the change is not going to end.

As managers in the tech industry, we need to lead our teams through constant, rapid change, whether it's technical, cultural, or business change. Our growth industry requires us to be comfortable with high ambiguity and rate of change.

We need to be able to solve problems, inspire, and motivate teams with positivity during change. This is challenging, often thankless work, that doesn't show up in performance reviews or Objectives and Key Results (OKRs). There's rarely training, so what can we do?

Here's a framework to help you lead teams through change. It has two components:

Time phase
Where is the company at in the change timeline?

Leadership qualities
What type of leadership does the company need?

Time Phase

There are three time phases that require different things from leaders:

Acute phase

The month or two following an event that typically triggers rapid change (because there almost always is one), such as hiring a new CTO, an acquisition, or closing a round of funding.

Rapid phase

The next and longest phase lasts several months. It is the period of predictably constant, rapid change. If you plot time on the x-axis and the number of changes on the y-axis, you see constant change growth.

New normal

When constant change begins to decelerate and plateau. In our growth industry, this means you've reached a (temporary) "new" normal.

Leadership Qualities

There are three leadership qualities that are most important when leading through change: *communication, motivation,* and *focus.* We need to optimize for them differently depending on the time phase we're in and what our company needs from us as leaders.

Communication

Managers need to overcommunicate during times of change and optimize for the exact balance of these methods:

- Use *one-way* (i.e., presentations) and *two-way* (i.e., small group Q&A) communications strategically
- Use the proper mix of both *written* and *in-person* communications
- Be as *transparent* as you can
- Provide enough *context* about why change is happening
- Actively *listen* and communicate in an *empathetic* way

Motivation

It's essential that managers keep teams highly motivated through rapid change. You can use these practices:

- Paint a picture of a company and software product that *inspires* everyone
- Emphasize *company values* to ground the team
- Make sure everyone understands the *company vision, mission, and strategy*

- Manage with the appropriate balance of *empowerment versus direction* because it will change
- Help your teams set clear goals so that they can *measure their impact*

Focus

It's so easy to lose focus during growth and change. Don't let it happen! Push yourself to do the following:

- Invest in *only the most important initiatives* even when it's easy to invest in more
- Continue to improve your ability to *execute and deliver*
- Become great at regularly *prioritizing and reprioritizing* the work

You can use this framework by thinking of a time of change you faced or are facing, and for each *time phase*, write down the *leadership qualities* that are most valuable for your company's specific situation. Doing this exercise as a retrospective can really help you learn from the past and come up with actionable things to try to do better next time. Doing this exercise as you're experiencing change can help you prioritize and organize your time so that you can lead your team positively through it.

For example, using this framework I did a retrospective of the year after my company was acquired and learned the following:

Acute phase

It's important to over-index on in-person, two-way, communication over other methods. I didn't see trust rebuild with my team until I did small group meetings with a lot of Q&A. In those, I could be transparent and provide nuanced context, and they could see I was really empathetic and listening to their concerns.

Rapid phase

We needed to periodically reset to the proper balance of empowerment versus direction in order to keep our cross-functional teams motivated and focused. As the company grew and changed, that balance frequently changed in different ways and we didn't reset it often enough.

New normal

A focus on execution and delivery of our key initiatives was critical, as was regularly prioritizing only the key initiatives. It's far too easy to become distracted.

Making Your New Team Feel Like a Team

Camille Fournier

Engineering is a team sport. Gone are the days of the lone software developer churning out code alone in their room. In most effective organizations, software is written by engineers who are acting in teams. We work in shared codebases, give each other code reviews, and even sometimes write code in pairs. Good managers of software teams understand that it is their job to create this collaborative environment. It's not enough to focus on one-on-one meetings and understanding people as individuals, you also must work with the team as a whole to make the group effective.

Learning how to do this takes time, and it is just as awkward to start as your early one-on-ones might feel. Here are some questions to answer as you begin:

- What is your team called? Naming is one of the most difficult problems in computer science, and spending some time on the name you give your team is a good thing to do. It forces you to succinctly describe the work that your team does, so try to resist the urge to name your team by obscure analogy. It's better to call yourself the Sales Engineering team rather than Team Glengarry. Naming is the first step in the long-running project of defining your team's mission.

- What are the processes that your team does together, as a group? You might follow some variant of an Agile methodology, which gives you an automatic baseline for bringing the team together to work. If you don't, you need to bring your team together regularly to discuss the work! If you're at a loss, I would recommend a regular quick standup meeting for briefly reviewing in-flight work and priorities, and periodic retrospectives to look back and talk about what went well and what could improve. No matter what you do, it is important that you bring your team together as a group to talk about the work on a regular cadence.

- Think about the roles that each team member plays with respect to the team as a whole. One person is the operations expert, whereas another is the architect. Jane is seen as the technical leader; Joe is the junior engineer. Where do the responsibilities of these roles overlap, and where are there gaps? You might discover that you need to hire for missing capabilities or cross-train people to ensure good coverage of important skills.

- How are you making sure that there is good knowledge sharing across members of the team? Code reviews are rarely enough. Consider having team members share their work by presenting it to the group, writing and discussing their designs, and sharing support responsibilities broadly.

Two things will begin to happen when you think about the team as a group. The first is that you'll be forced to pay attention to how your team works together. If there are two members who cannot work together, that is something that you must address. On a team of 10 or fewer people, having two people who are in deep conflict is a problem for the team's health and something you need to take seriously.

The second is that you'll begin to see that the way your team works together contributes greatly to the happiness of its members. Thinking of the team as a system itself instead of just a grouping of individuals can help you avoid one of the common early management traps, which is micro-optimizing for individual happiness over the strength of the team. Individual engineers don't always know what will make them happy and often overvalue the things they can easily understand, like hard technical challenges or promotions. Your job is to make sure the team doesn't neglect things that are more difficult to understand but cause longer-term happiness, like being able to release their code frequently.

This transition to thinking beyond individuals and about the team as a whole is stressful. There can be a lag between making changes that benefit the entire team and seeing the value of those changes. The first time you need to disappoint an individual in favor of the team's overall needs is tough. For the long-term well-being of the group, it is critical that you think about the team as your first order of business. So, give it a name, make sure it meets regularly, and get everyone working together, and you'll be on the road to a high-performing team.

Manage Complexity with Diversity

Mike Fisher

As engineering managers, we often develop and manage complex systems that have interacting components (people, process, technology), the combination of which make it very difficult to predict the outcome from simply observing the inputs. Additionally, many of the subsystems are tightly coupled in that a failure of one can result in cascading failures. As such, managing the inherent risk associated with these complex systems is a daunting task.

Decades of research into the management of complex systems has given us normal accident theory, high reliability, and the logic of failure, just to name a few. Organizational design based on high reliability even identifies five characteristics of organizations that are best to deal with complexity: preoccupation with failure, reluctance to simplify interpretations, sensitivity to unexpected conditions, commitment to resilience, and deference to experts. The logic of failure identifies ways to fail in the decision-making process, including failing to prioritize goals, using overly reductive models, and failing to generate alternative plans. However, only recently have researchers turned their focus to the makeup of the organization instead of its behavioral characteristics and processes.

Research has begun to catch up with what savvy practitioners have long known, that diverse teams are better able to manage complex systems. "Groupthink" is a very real phenomenon that plagues teams that are composed of a cohesive group of individuals who share many similar characteristics. Our willingness to disagree in a group increases dramatically if the group is diverse. Homogeneity might facilitate smooth and effortless interactions, but diversity drives better decisions. Interestingly, it's the diversity and not necessarily the specific contributions of the individuals themselves that causes greater skepticism, more open and active dialogue, and less group-think.

Healthy skepticism is incredibly useful in myriad situations. One such situation is during premortems, in which a project team imagines that a project has failed and works to identify what potentially could lead to such an outcome. This is very different from a postmortem, in which the failure has already occurred and the team is dissecting the failure. Often, individuals who have been working on projects for weeks or more are biased with overconfidence that the project will be successful. The premortem exercise can help ameliorate these biases, especially when diverse team members participate.

Another benefit of having a diverse team is the culture of inclusivity that it helps to develop. Even though recruiting or large compensation packages might bring in diverse candidates, those candidates will stay only if the culture is inclusive enough to value them and their contributions. Having an inclusive culture trains engineers and managers to listen to one another and drop the preconceived notions about someone's knowledge or ideas. During a crisis or incident, having a team whose culture is open and inclusive allows them to accept ideas from many viewpoints. This results in more creative problem solving and faster resolution of issues.

Managing complex systems can be a daunting task for any engineering manager, but there are strategies that many of us have relied on to help. One of the most effective that I've found is surrounding yourself with a great team of people, and that means a diverse team. When our teams comprise diverse members, we make better decisions, build better products, and manage complex systems better.

Management Is a Different Set of APIs

Raquel Vélez

When folks ask me what engineering management is like, I boil it down to three things:

1. Unfortunately, as you probably already know, people. (I stole this from a sign in my old office. It featured a horse knitting a scarf that said "Oakland." The quote originally came from @horse_ebooks on Twitter.)

2. Management is *not* a promotion. It's a career change.

3. It's a lot like engineering, if you abstract it out enough.

Let's dig into #3.

I want you to imagine that a person is a service. (This will be easier if you have worked at a company with a service-oriented architecture. If you've worked only at companies with monolith codebases, consider them a function with multiple parameters and extrapolate from there.)

This person-service gets spun up upon joining your team. You don't control the box; you control only the environment in which it resides. Your first task is to learn the API required to send and receive data from this box.

For sending, it might take some time before you figure out just the exact parameters and payloads to send. *This is perfectly normal.* You can reduce the time to first "Hello World" by reading the documentation (e.g., asking questions): learn about the person-service. Sometimes, person-services are self-aware enough to know what works and what doesn't. Sometimes, person-services are brand new and there are some unknowns, even to themselves. When this happens, congratulations! You get to be part of the person-service's scaling and growth. It's very exciting.

For receiving, note that your person-service will send you information that you need to parse. In many ways, your person-service will be doing the same sending exercise with you that you did with them: they'll be trying to figure out your API, as well. The more self-aware you are, the better your documentation can be: answer questions and set expectations.

After you understand the API for sending information, use it wisely. Be really clear about your expectations. Remember that conflict arises when expectations don't meet reality. Most often, this is due to an API mismatch: perhaps your person-service isn't sending very useful error codes. Perhaps your person-service isn't aware of the difference between a 301 and a 302. Perhaps you've forgotten major parts of the payload body; you received a 200, but the return payload is empty because the person-service thought you were sending a status update instead of instructions.

Your role as the person-cluster manager is to ensure that all of your person-services are sending, receiving, and performing as expected. (Not just with you, but with the other services in the cluster, as well!) Newer person-services will need more handholding, whereas older person-services might require some low-level maintenance.

I highly recommend creating Service-Level Objectives, indicators, and agreements for your person-services, as well. A good set of logs and dashboards will help you and your person-services understand overall performance. Check in on each of your person-services once each week to review performance, set expectations, and plan for future scaling. This time is also a good opportunity to improve APIs, review load, and discuss external factors that might be affecting day-to-day efficiencies.

Finally, upgrades are a fun but potentially fraught time: work closely with your person-services to ensure that it's done at a time that is mutually beneficial. Too soon and your person-service might not have sufficient hardware to keep up with the new responsibilities. Too late and your person-service might tire out before you have a chance to upgrade.

This brings me to #1 on my aforementioned list: services are a great abstraction, but they're not quite right. And that's because people are messy. Humans are squishy, with feelings. They have fears and dreams, doubts and excitement. An API endpoint that worked yesterday might suddenly change today. Spinning a new service up is exciting; spinning a service down is far more devastating in people-land than in a cluster. Acknowledge this from the outset, and you will thank yourself later.

Which brings me to #2 (who goes in order, anyway?): management is in no way a promotion. Prepare to go back to feeling like a junior developer: every day you will get nominally better, but you will make mistakes regularly. If you're lucky, you'll knock out some of the basics early on. If you're like most folks, you'll make a massive mistake when you least expect it. This is totally normal and expected.

Good luck!

Manager Handoffs

Lara Hogan

Think about the history you have built with your direct reports. You're aware of their current goals, and how they came to be. You have background. You have context. You've *been there* for their career accomplishments, their failures, their moments of needing clear and actionable feedback. You've likely been the person to share with them news about change within the organization, and you've steered the ship of your team so far.

So, when someone gets a new manager, it can feel like starting over—their relationship and trust with their new manager needs to be built from scratch, and their career momentum might stall. One of folks' core needs at work is to have a sense of improvement or progress toward a goal; this could be a goal for the organization, for their team, or for themselves personally. And when they lose their manager and get a new one, it's easy to feel like this sense of improvement or progress forward is about to be threatened.

If managers care to do a handoff for their direct reports at all, *most* will have it behind closed doors. This means that direct reports will have no idea what was discussed, whether everything important was captured, and—the scariest bit—whether their former manager represented things accurately.

When you're in this situation, try a new twist on manager handoffs: a "one-on-one-on-one." A one-on-one is between a manager and their direct report; a one-on-one-on-one includes both the former manager *and* the new manager. this is an opportunity to ensure that direct reports' career momentum doesn't experience that hiccup.

The goals of a one-on-one-on-one are to do the following:

- Share relevant information between managers about the direct report's feedback, projects, growth areas, and goals.

- Do this transparently so that the direct report can disagree or clarify when there's important things going unsaid or things that differ from their own perception.
- Reduce the natural career friction, pausing, or hiccups that happen when a person gets a new manager.

This is an opportunity to turn an otherwise lossy process into a much more thorough, supportive process for a direct report. This is awkward because the direct report is sitting right there, listening! But this awkwardness is in service of clarity and fully supporting the direct report's career path, which can otherwise be muddled in manager changes or cause plenty of friction, confusion, or angst in the future.

During the one-on-one-on-one, state the goal: to make sure you and the new manager are transparent in the handoff of this direct report's career, how they want to grow, and the best ways that their new manager can support them. Highlight that this meeting is also an opportunity for your direct report to agree/disagree with how these things are characterized.

I know that this can be super uncomfortable, but as much as possible, be transparent and honest as you share the following:

- Their most recent review cycle feedback
- More recent feedback, projects, and other relevant info since that last review cycle
- Their growth areas and other career-related things for their new manager to know

The new manager should ask questions as the handoff progresses. You should both be optimizing for gaining a shared understanding of this person's history, goals, work, and so on.

If the direct report is quiet, the managers in the room should be routinely asking things like this:

- How do you feel so far about what's been said?
- Does this description match your experience?
- Are we missing something on that topic?
- Anything we should clarify?
- Anything you disagree with?

I've seen this be a super-boring meeting in which everything is clear and agreed upon. I've seen this get sticky and uncomfortable when a direct report has an opposing viewpoint or different recollection. As necessary, acknowledge out loud that it's okay if this is awkward. If it gets to a point where the dialog isn't productive anymore, the new manager should talk with the direct report separately and privately about their experience. It's totally natural that the former manager and direct report have different perceptions of the same events or feedback—we're humans, which means this stuff is messy. Where it helps, restate those original meeting goals.

More often than not, even when things become uncomfortable, it's still a productive use of everyone's time, and it starts the new reporting relationship off on a much healthier foot. It will be quicker for the new manager and direct report to form a trusting relationship. And, hopefully, the direct report's future promotion process, trajectory toward goals, and work continues with the same momentum.

Managers and Culture

Arjun Anand

When I was pursuing my engineering degree, there were these hazing rituals in which those from a higher year bullied those of us who were just arriving. When I asked one of the seniors why they wanted to bully and haze us, he said that they do it because it was done to them. I never did get hazed, and so I never knew what that feeling was like, and so I never hazed anyone who was my junior either. What's funny to me is that we still do this now even when we're older and working in professional careers; we just call it the organization's culture.

In an organization, the people who your employees will turn to in order to see the "preferred interpretation" of the company's culture are the managers, leaders, and executives. These individuals are the day-to-day representation of any organization's culture, and thus, it is imperative for the success of an organization to set the tone for leadership. To this end, I wanted to share a few thoughts that I feel are important for a leader in an organization (as well as for the organization itself) to know in order to support and grow new leaders.

Manager Training

When moving someone along the management career path, it is important to understand where they've come from, what they want to achieve, and how it aligns with the organization's goals so that you can create plans for them. Training doesn't mean just providing good reading material; it means having learning events to teach managers good habits, cultivate the appropriate skills for their levels, and providing safe avenues of practice. This manager training is what will make the difference between your employees thriving or leaving in apathy.

Failure as a Rite of Passage

Although as an individual contributor you are able to be more in control of the individual tasks that you have assigned to you, as a manager you are responsible for making your reports work efficiently, all the while keeping them happy. In doing this you will fail many times. How your organization responds to your shortcomings will dictate how you react to your direct reports. It best serves an organization to help the manager learn from their shortcomings so they can learn that this is what they should do for their direct reports, too.

Keeping Things Professional

One of the most difficult things to do when you step into a manager's role for the first time is understanding when you should be a friend and when you should be a manager. This is an important trait to develop because at times there will be circumstances in which you must decide between being nice to a friend or being impartial in critiquing an employee's work. If not handled properly, it can potentially lead to the manager feeling a crisis in their ability to execute their job effectively, and you might end up losing some great employees and managers.

Conflict Resolution

When you put multiple people into any room, you now have multiple personalities, each with unique traits, thoughts, opinions, and ways of working. Depending on the pressures of the work, things will at some point begin to conflict. It is thus important for an organization to train the managers to deal with these situations. They need to be aware of when they need to step in and intervene, when and how to give feedback to the individuals involved in the conflict, when to take an unbiased stand, and when to escalate it, as well.

Coming to Terms with Your Skills

One of the most difficult things to do in professional life is performing an honest self-assessment; not for the organization during appraisal time, but for yourself to assess whether what you're doing makes you happy. A good leader motivates people, looks for ways to unblock them, mentors them, and guides them through problems, and also recognizes when they are not the right person for the job. Accepting this as a reality will give you and your organization the opportunity to deal with it properly and set an example for future managers who go down the same path.

Culture and management go hand in hand in any organization. How an organization defines its culture and cultivates its managers and seniors is what will define whether these individuals in turn will create an environment in which employees will be able to thrive and be creative, or an environment in which following the status quo and bullying/being bullied become the norm. In either case, it is important to remember the adage, "People leave bosses, not companies." Also true is, "People stick to bosses, not companies."

Monuments and Hamburgers

Travis Donia

Work is often allocated based on *CapEx* and *OpEx* budgets. These allocations can happen via the organization chart, as a separate career ladder for engineers who are developing new products and features versus those who maintain software that's already been deployed. In other types of organizations, the same team might do both, and it will fall on an engineering manager to help classify the expenses. In those cases, you might field questions from the finance department asking whether you can CapEx this project or set up a time tracker. It's easy to brush these topics aside as bureaucracy, but by investigating how they work in your organization, they can help you to understand the business case for your team's work. As a manager, becoming familiar with that business case and understanding the budget that funds your team will help you take on more ambitious initiatives.

First, some background. CapEx, or *capital expenditures*, are costs that go toward the creation of an asset that holds lasting value. Think of a monument. These are treated as an expense that is spread across the expected life of the asset. Sure, that pyramid cost us a lot to build, but it's something we can amortize across thousands of years, so our cost per year is low. There are standards for whether an expense qualifies: it must already be feasible, and management must have explicitly allocated resources to it in advance. These expenses are omitted from the EBITDA, the standard measure of the company's performance, and are treated as investments on the company's balance sheet. They also have a different tax treatment, which is why your finance team cares about them when they're closing the books for a quarter or year. They are also the type of investments that certain investors—especially venture capitalists—chase because they believe in the strategic value a new technology will create.

Operating expenditures (OpEx), are the opposite of a capital investment. When you're in the business of making a consumable product, like hamburgers, you hope they will be delivered in the same fiscal year. Most of the cost of that burger is OpEx. These costs are included in the EBITDA and are important when evaluating the business operating margin, signaling how profitable the business is.

Software is a famously high-margin business. After your team develops the product, it can be sold for the cost of distributing it, which is almost nothing on the internet. This dynamic also implies that product roles are predicated on there being a continuous stream of projects that will yield a positive ROI for the company either by reducing costs or driving revenue growth. Beware of CapEx roles at a company that's decided to stop innovating. Here's how Google talks about CapEx in its annual report to investors:

> **As we continue to look for new ways to serve our users and expand our businesses, we will invest heavily in R&D and our capital expenditures will continue to fluctuate.**
>
> We continue to make significant research and development (R&D) investments in areas of strategic focus such as advertising, cloud, machine learning, and search, as well as in new products and services. The amount of our capital expenditures has fluctuated and may continue to fluctuate in the long term as we invest heavily in our systems, data centers, real estate and facilities, and information technology infrastructure.

Whenever you can eliminate a substantial recurring operating expense with a one-time CapEx project, you can create value, so as an engineering leader, it makes sense to identify, execute, and deliver CapEx projects.

The opposite strategy can also be effective. Amazon Web Services (AWS) lets millions of companies shift what were once large CapEx investments in datacenters and hardware into more bite-size OpEx rental fees for their "cloud." Of course, Amazon's own profit margin on this business comes from its ability to make the CapEx that it's investing into your OpEx, and to amortize that investment across as many customers as possible. This idea underpins the rise of SaaS companies: if you can take what was a substantial CapEx investment for your customers and instead meter it based on usage in a given year, the waste that's reduced and the risk eliminated will create a significant ROI.

For anyone who started their career as a freelancer, your core unit of work was the "project," which was probably someone else's CapEx investment. The maintenance and hosting fees were OpEx. Every business has this dynamic. The language is a little more *Investopedia* and a little less *Knuth*, but your ability to become fluent enough to use it will help you to understand how the market measures your performance. You can begin by identifying where your budget appears in the company's balance sheet.

Thank you to Stephanie Wai for reading and editing drafts of this essay.

Navigating the Bumpy Road from Engineer to Manager

Jean Hsu

The transition from engineer to engineering manager is *rough*.

Coding is a fairly objective process, or at least it's treated like one. Many companies track the crude metrics of number of lines of code added or number of commits. The path to seniority is fairly clear in terms of the work—building, debugging, maintaining, and being a core contributor for larger and larger projects. There are some nuances, but generally speaking, at the end of the day, if you've had a big chunk of heads-down coding time, and merged a handful of pull requests, it was a good day. Most of the uncertainty around the technical path comes not from the work itself but from titles, compensation, and perceived career progression.

Managing people and teams is a much more subjective process, so much so that companies routinely try to have "no managers—a completely flat organization!" A lot of management is the less-visible things, and the default feedback loop for these are much longer. Progression along this path is much more unknown.

No wonder the transition is so difficult. Most first-time managers don't get any support. Many senior engineers decide to move back to the hands-on technical work after a few years of managing people and teams—you might hear, "never again" or "management wasn't for me, I just want to code." A large swath of questions and blog posts around moving to engineering management are more or less variations of:

> How do I keep my technical edge?

This question is symptomatic of a more fundamental problem, which is that these first-time engineering managers are not getting guidance in seeing the impact and rewards of moving into a management role.

Dealing with the anxiety and sense of being unproductive, of course they grasp at and gravitate to the much more objectively rewarding work of coding.

So, how can we pave the road so that it's not as bumpy? Making that transition smoothly requires a fundamental mindset shift in how you view your own productivity and self-worth. If you are someone in this transition, keep reading to explore some ways to make it smoother.

Self: Keep a Log

At the end of each day, jot down the most impactful thing you did that day. Let yourself generously speculate about possible downstream effects. It can help highlight the potential impact of your actions when things seem very chaotic and uncertain.

Example: Today I had a meaningful one-on-one with Alice and helped her see how important her work is to the team's purpose and overall goals. The increased alignment could make her more motivated and productive, which might increase team morale, as well.

Example: Bob came to me with an interpersonal issue that he was struggling with. I coached him to give feedback in a kind way. He pinged me on Slack in the afternoon that the conversation had gone really well. Now he has that skill in his toolbelt for future challenging situations. And he has one successful example in which he took initiative to change something that's not working.

Internal: Find Peer Support

One or a group of trusted peers can act as a sounding board.

Being able to post something like, "Hey, I have this situation, and here's how I'm thinking of approaching it. Am I missing anything?" in a confidential setting is extremely valuable. Senior managers can coach first-time managers, and first-time managers can commiserate together and then help one another through the rough times. Peer support in a company—someone you can reach out to and say, "Do you have 10 min? I want to run something by you"—is ideal. At smaller companies, this is often not possible, so having an explicit external peer relationship can also be very useful, especially for sharing best practices and perspectives across companies.

External: Work with a Coach

As an engineering leadership coach, my job is not to convince people that management is or isn't the way forward. A good coach can shine a light on someone's strengths, areas for improvement, and the rewards and impact of that management path so that they can make an informed decision. Many potentially great managers go back to primarily IC work because of inadequate support, and they don't have anyone to bring the management path into as clear a focus as the technical path.

The path can be dark and bumpy at times, but having grounding anchors of support can set you up for the journey ahead while you get your footing.

The New Way to Manage by Walking Around

Yvette Pasqua

Since the 1970s, some of the most successful managers at tech companies have used a practice called "management by walking around" (MBWA) to build stronger communication channels, gather information and feedback, and reduce inefficiencies. The origin is traced back to the management practices at Hewlett-Packard and was made popular in the bestseller, *In Search of Excellence: Lessons from America's Best Run Companies*. Steve Jobs and his team used the practice extensively at Apple.

The ultimate goal of MBWA is to improve a manager's ability to learn to make better decisions and solve problems for their team. Here are the key practices that the manager adopts:

- Systematically and regularly get up and out of their office and talk to their employees.

- Start ad hoc conversations so that they can gather information and feedback, hear the perspective of their employees, and identify and stay on top of problems.

- Create network within the organization to encourage stronger relationships and open communication throughout the whole organization.

Today, the goals of MBWA are still critical to a manager's success, but we need to evolve past old MBWA practices for the following reasons:

- Most managers don't have offices and are already sitting with their teams.

- Engineers struggle to focus in an open office. Walking around and starting ad hoc conversations interrupts a maker's flow and hurts productivity.

- Networks within organizations have changed. Most communication and relationship building happens digitally in real time. The workforce is increasingly more distributed with remote employees the norm.

So, what does an engineering manager do who wants to accomplish the goals of MBWA today?

Use real-time messaging (i.e., Slack)

This is an efficient tool to broadly and systematically gather information and talk with your employees without interrupting their maker flow. It's a great tool for creating networks within the organization to encourage stronger relationships and open communication. To use it effectively:

- *Join a broad and large number of channels* and systematically read them (one to two times per day) so that you can gather as much information as possible.

- Create a system and culture where *creating public channels to build company networks* is the norm, to foster frequent and open communication within and across those networks.

- *Communicate in channels deliberately.* Reward loudly and publicly the culture and results you want to see. When you see problems, offer support and help in a safe way, and show that you're listening and taking action.

Set up one-on-one meetings

Use these to gather information and feedback, hear the perspective of others, and identify and stay on top of problems. In-person communications uncover things that you never would otherwise learn, and they build a foundation for deeper relationships. Some best practices to support this use case include:

- *Don't just hold regular one-on-ones with your direct reports.* Set up skip levels, one-on-ones with your peers, and others in different networks across the company.

- *Create a safe space* for people to talk about difficult things, bring up problems, and ask for help. Show your own vulnerability and talk about your own problems. Make discussions confidential by default unless you explicitly ask someone if you can share something in order to help them.

- *Ask direct and open-ended questions* and then actively listen. Become really good at reading the subtle signs people tell you with body language or tone. If you suspect that there might be more they're not telling you, follow up with related direct and open-ended questions and wait through uncomfortable silence as they figure out how to say something they've wanted to say but aren't sure how to.

- *Take action quickly.* Be transparent about your actions so that you preserve the safe space and trust. Ask them, "Is it OK if I take action on this by speaking with this person about this thing?"

Write weekly emails/posts

This is an excellent way to model and foster open communication throughout the entire organization and communicate decisions.

- *Write about specific things you worked on,* important results, and things you want to share and reinforce. Write about problems often. The more specific and authentic, the better because you'll build trust and a culture of open communication.

- *Send it to as broad an audience as you feel comfortable with* so you can align everyone and model open communications. This includes your team, across your peer group (other managers at your level), and up (your manager and their peers).

- *Include explicit and easy ways for people to speak with you* and push information to you. For example, include a link for people to sign up for office hours or invite them to email or write to you via a Slack channel.

Not Everyone Wants to Be a People Manager

Jesse Anderson

Occasionally, technical people get pushed into management. This can be good—sometimes technical people need coaxing into getting out of their comfort zone and into something new. This also can be bad—such as when a technical person really doesn't want to be a people manager.

These forced promotions often come when companies lack a promotion path for their technical tracks. For example, their lead software engineer is incredible, but there is nowhere to promote that person. The company lacks a technical individual contributor title—and pay grade—above some kind of arbitrary limit.

Looking around they find the need to promote that person into management and that's when the problems begin. I've seen this firsthand a few times and spoken to the individuals who find themselves in a management position that they never wanted or should be in.

This is when the individual begins to feel stuck. I've known people whose promotion to manager was publicly announced before they were even asked whether they wanted to be manager. I've had people realize early on that management wasn't for them, but the title and social praise kept them in the position.

It's sad because these people feel there's no other way out of the problem. They're faced with choosing the lesser of three evils: toughing it out, transferring within the company, or quitting the company. More often than not, the person feels the need to quit to save face and move back into an individual contributor position. The quitting part is really a blow to the organization. The person was promoted because they were a great individual contributor and now the organization lost them.

Whether you're on the receiving end of an unwanted promotion or you're looking for a technical person to promote, the same solution exists: you need to communicate (this will come in handy while you're managing!). This is a time when you should ask questions like these:

- Is going into management one of your goals?
- Is the reason you're needing or wanting to go into management because there isn't a technical individual contributor path that goes high enough?
- Given the choice between staying an individual contributor or a manager, which would you choose?
- Are you afraid or leery of going into management because it's something new?

When dealing with this fear, sometimes people will try to manage and code. I tried this and it just doesn't work. I did both jobs poorly. Sitting in meetings all day or trying to code in between meetings just leaves you set up for failure.

It's really a Gordian Knot that you need to cut. I wasn't ready to hang up my keyboard and I thought I could do both. I couldn't. I should have done one or the other. I eventually did cut that knot and did much better as a direct result.

If I could do it again, I would ease into the position more. I would understand what it meant to be a *good* manager rather than what *I* thought was a good manager (there's even a book about that now). I would spend time looking outside my limited network to find those who truly exemplified and practiced good management skills. I think I based too much of my management style on the (comparatively poor) management styles that had been modeled to me by my previous managers. I would remember that management isn't just about running meetings and scrums. Finally, I would focus on continuous improvement instead of just continuous learning.

On Accountability

Jason Wong

Accountability comes up a lot when talking about engineering organizations. Everyone wants to know how to hold engineers accountable. In my exploration of this topic with folks, I've found that the term *accountability* means something different to everyone. There are some folks who use accountability to mean an ability to explain. There's a slightly larger set of people who use accountability when they really mean ownership. And then, there are a large number of organizations that use accountability to mean a mechanism to blame and punish people when they "don't perform."

This topic is difficult because discussions on accountability so often originate from an implicit, forgone conclusion. Something is going wrong at my company, let me roll out some accountability measures to prove that X team is not doing their job. Accountability becomes an externalization mechanism that very conveniently directs a leader's problems outward rather than inward, skipping over the people with the most influence on an outcome: the leaders.

I talk a lot about the importance of alignment and contextualizing problems in my management practice. The idea is that communication is key, as is building narratives around why a project is important for the company and why it should matter to my engineers. The idea is that you can avoid a whole host of problems just by having a story, a "vision, mission, strategy, objectives" statement or some narrative arc that aligns and motivates your team.

People initially gobble this up. I get a lot of head nods and "mmm hmms." But rarely do I get out of these conversations without someone asking, "But how do you hold people accountable?" And, I kind of stumble here, because, often times what's behind that question is an insinuation that people are operating with bad intent. But in the past seven years of my experience, that has rarely happened. Does it happen? Yes. And usually, having a chat with that person is enough to get them moving. Sometimes, that chat is friendly. Sometimes, that chat is what we in the biz call a "difficult conversation."

One of the uncomfortable truths about the vast majority of the work we do in tech is that it is rarely the case that people aren't technically capable of doing the work. It is far more common that people disagree about what the work is and the parties involved have some constraint that prevents reconciliation, whether it be time, ability to repair misunderstandings, or desire to come to an agreement. Folks aren't fired because they can't do the job. They're fired because the people involved can't get to an understanding of what the job is and, in the process of hashing it out, have torn their relationship to shreds.

Which brings me to a couple ideas. The first is that accountability is a capability, not a measure. It is a means and not an end. Having or creating accountability will not solve your team or organizational performance problems. It will give you the ability to understand your performance problems, and how you address them is up to you.

The second is that if most of your conversations around your engineering team are about needing accountability because your engineering organization is underperforming, that is more of a reflection on the leadership than it is on the team. Maybe you are hiring the wrong people. Maybe the team doesn't have the ability to do the work. But, most of the dysfunction I've seen comes from some flavor of lack of goal clarity. Whether that is failure to define the goal, rapidly changing the goal, having too many goals, or not having a strong story about why achieving the goal is important. Whatever the reasons end up being, there's rarely a world in which you as a leader didn't have a hand in creating the environment in which those problems have been able to persist. So, whatever definition of accountability you're using, the first place to apply it is to yourself and your leadership team.

Finally, if you still believe accountability is your number one problem, try something Lara Hogan recommends: using more descriptive words to clarify what you mean. Do you mean that you want a system to be able to punish or reward people? Do you want the ability to create clear lines of responsibility? Or, do you need to be able to find the folks who can answer all of your topic-area questions? Whatever it is, being unambiguous from the start will help everyone involved.

On the Elusiveness of Time in Tracking Progress

Mathias Meyer

When I started my very first job out of university, I was assigned to a project that already had a predefined list of tasks and estimates. None of these I had been involved in setting.

At the end of every week I sent my manager a progress report, stating how many hours I had worked on a task from the project plan and how much longer I thought it would take to finish that task. Everything was okay as long as I sent back numbers that exactly aligned with the plan.

Engineers know from experience that estimates tend to be used as targets rather than guesses. They tend to be set in stone after they're established. And yet we also know that things tend to take longer than we expect them to.

As humans we err toward optimistic estimates. Yet as managers, many of us tend to fall back to the same pattern. We look at time spent working or how long someone was in the office as our means of measuring progress.

Time is easy to reason about. Based on an estimate and time spent on a project so far, we can come up with a specific number of how much time we're going to spend until it's finished. The assumption then holds that when the time was used up, the project or task will be done.

This is a mistake that I'm seeing many managers make, especially when they're new to management. Another mistake they tend to make is thinking that if your engineers do work more hours, you'll still achieve the goal.

This might work in the short term, but in the long term, you'll burn out your team. They'll end up leaving the company if things don't improve, if you don't improve. Working overtime is a short-term fix, and it should be a last resort. Otherwise, it's damaging not just to your organization, it's damaging to your people.

Measuring progress in time is a focus on output. It's similar to lines of code. It tells you that work might have been done, or rather that time has passed that you expect was spent productively and exclusively working on that task.

This is rarely the reality. Meetings, impromptu conversations, changing priorities, and unplanned work tend to creep up on engineers all the time. It's not an inherently bad thing that they do, it just happens.

Writing code is an inherently creative activity. It requires thinking about a problem, building prototypes to verify assumptions, and adjusting course when those assumptions aren't met.

Experienced engineers learn how to get their estimates closer and closer to reality. But as humans, we fall on the side of being too optimistic when it comes to predicting the future and guessing how long something is going to take.

How do you get past using time as the sole indicator of progress? How can you make sure, as the manager, that you're on top of your team's progress?

The most difficult activity you'll need to do with your team is to break down the work. For any project, no matter how long, be deliberate about breaking the work down into smaller pieces. Allow your team to verify assumptions quickly and have a regular discussion about progress.

For each week, set goals with your team of what they'd like to achieve. Check in with them in the middle of the week on how confident they are as to whether they're going to reach those goals. A 1-to-10 scale is sufficient, unless you're German or Swiss; in which case, go for 0 to 100%. If they're not confident, ask them why and adjust as needed.

At the end of each week, review your progress. Did you achieve your goals? If so, keep going! If not, what got in the way? Were those goals too optimistic? Adjust your goals for the next weeks based on what you've learned. Repeat this every week.

As time is an unavoidable part of working in a business, keep in mind that there are two more knobs available to you as a manager: quality and scope. If time is a fixed variable—for instance, a fixed launch date—be diligent and ruthless to cut down scope or to adjust quality as much as is bearable for the business and your team.

Even though your customers and stakeholders like to say that neither quality nor scope are negotiable, they always are. It's your task as a manager to do everything you can to negotiate on them.

Onboard People, Not Technology

Marcus Blankenship

At my first programming job, it took three weeks to get my dev environment fully set up. I was only the second developer to work at the company, ever, so nothing was documented. The first person quit, which is why I had the job. At my second job, it took only four days because I was the eighth person in the programming department, so I had seven other people to help me. Today, my clients tell me things like, "we use Docker, so it takes less than an hour to onboard a new developer."

I'm glad new devs don't need to face the same frustrations that I did. But setting up a productive dev environment isn't onboarding. Onboarding is setting up a person to work productively on your team.

A Leadership Smell

Some managers might fall into the trap of believing that after they're done setting up the dev environment, they've done their part to make the new developer successful and that the rest is up to the new employee, that all they need is a computer, a chair, a dev environment, and a project to work on.

This is a dangerous leadership smell. Dangerous for the manager, yes, but mostly for the new developer.

The danger is the unspoken idea that after we apply onboarding to a new developer, they have everything they need to be productive. Of course, when you read it, it seems sort of ridiculous.

But I get a whiff of this from managers at many organizations I work with. It typically comes out in a conversation like this:

> Me: How is your new programmer working out?
>
> Manager: He's doing…okay. Not quite what I hoped, but he'll be fine.

Me: What makes you say that?

Manager: Well, we got everything set up quickly, and we got him all his access and onboarding. But he's just a lot slower than I expected.

Me: Why did you expect he'd be faster?

Manager: First, he was supposed to be an expert in Java development. Second, we've automated our dev environment setup at great cost and effort. So, there shouldn't be anything standing in his way.

As you might guess, this situation is more dangerous for the programmer than the manager, because it's the manager's expectations that aren't being met. It's the manager who's disappointed by the speed at which things are progressing. And it's the manager who feels that their onboarding process, whatever it is, should yield a developer that's "up to speed and ready to run."

So, if the manager believes they've done their part, the problem must be with the developer's motivation, drive, or skill. This ignores the most important keys to productivity: good relationships and a healthy environment.

These are the things your developer needs to be onboarded to, and it takes much longer than just a few hours.

Onboarding Is Leading

Onboarding is a key activity of technical managers and leaders. It's not the responsibility of HR, and it's certainly not simply setting up the dev environment.

In my experience, onboarding should include or result in the following:

- Positive relationships with the developer's team
- Introductions to the project stakeholders
- Clarity about the team's current goals
- Knowledge of key upcoming projects
- Clarity about the team's values
- Knowing who to go to for help and how often it's okay to ask for help
- Firsthand experience with the team's development process and ceremonies (Agile, Scrum, standups, retros, etc.)
- Firsthand experience with the key communication channels (team meetings, one-on-ones, etc.)

- Receiving a piece of adjusting and affirming feedback from their manager
- Giving a piece of adjusting and affirming feedback to their manager and teammates
- A clear sense of the tech and infrastructure used by the team
- A working dev environment

How Long Should This Take?

It should take you, the manager, at least a few weeks to initially onboard a new developer. After that, expect it to take a few quarters (three to nine months) for a new developer to "come up to speed."

Of course, this will vary wildly according to the kind of projects you are working on. I've led teams where I spent a year onboarding a dev to work on a large ERP system. You might have experienced even longer.

Onboarding is important leadership work that you need to be actively involved with. Like other work, you don't need to do it all yourself, but you need to make sure it all gets done—and done well. Onboarding sets the stage for many years of productive work. Don't shortchange your team by pretending it's just about tools, paperwork, or diversity videos. It's about intentionally getting the proper relationships in place from day one, which is the key to productive development teams.

Onboarding Beyond Codelabs

Jean Hsu

When we think about onboarding process, we often think about codelabs, classes, and tutorials. And let's face it, at most high-growth startups, it can never seem like the right time to spin up a project to build out more onboarding resources.

Many years ago, I implemented two subtle but powerful changes to Medium's onboarding process. Surprisingly, neither is engineering specific nor have to do with code walkthroughs or tutorials at all. I share them with you here, along with a third bonus tip for building alignment quickly with a new member of your team.

First Impression

The first day of a new job can be daunting, overwhelming, and anxiety inducing—so no matter how much other onboarding classes or codelabs or dev environment setup documents you have in place, one of the highest impact ways you can put someone at ease is the first impression they have when they show up for work.

I set the first impression with a beautiful welcome letter on their desk. Every time a new engineer joined, I customized their welcome letter, printed it out on high-quality cardstock, and signed it with a pen, "Welcome! ~Medium Engineering."

The letter expressed the team's enthusiasm at their joining, followed by a beautifully formatted schedule of their first day. I included the name of their onboarding buddy (see the next tip) as well as a pointer to a guide to set up their dev environments to work on in between meetings.

This practice was soon adopted by the rest of the company. In a day of overwhelming new accounts, new people, laptop setup, and calendar invites for onboarding events for the next week or so, a simple and personal reference to what they need to feel welcome and get through that first day is key.

Onboarding Buddy

The biggest inconsistency I found across different engineers' onboarding experiences was whether they had adequate access to someone to whom they could ask any question.

The most impactful change I made to the onboarding process was to assign every new hire an *onboarding buddy*, who they were seated next to (if not remote). After they agreed to be a buddy, I'd send them an email detailing their responsibilities. Their highest priority for the first two to three weeks was to be available to the new hire to answer questions, pair-program, direct them to the appropriate people, and so on. I also required that on the new hire's first day, the buddy have a conversation with the new engineer, making that priority explicit. "My highest priority is getting you up to speed, so even if I look busy, feel free to ask me questions any time. Even if I don't know the answer, I can point you to the right person."

The onboarding buddy significantly reduced the barrier to asking for help. Getting someone set up and up to speed in days instead of weeks helps put them on a trajectory to be successful for their time at the company.

Powerful Questions to Build Alignment

As companies grow, they begin to codify their onboarding processes to scale with the scaling engineering team. But there is no one-size-fits-all; one engineer might thrive under light supervision, whereas another needs more guidance and guardrails.

What became clear to me is that in all the conversations about building onboarding processes, there was very little about how differently individuals learn—how some *like* to be thrown into the deep end with a meaty project, and some like to have their hands held for a few days before leaving the nest.

Ask a few of these powerful questions early on, and the answers might surprise you:

- What would be your ideal onboarding experience?
- What's a time when you felt really excited and motivated on a new project and team? What about it was most motivating?

- What does being supported at work look like for you?

Of course, as your team scales, you'll also add more standard onboarding resources. Those things are all important, but they also take a lot more time. These three tips I shared here—creating an inviting first impression, setting up an onboarding buddy system, and having an upfront conversation to discover what successful onboarding looks like for each new hire—don't require much time to implement, are extremely high leverage, and can really effectively smooth out some of the bumps as your team grows.

Own the Narrative

Adam Baratz

"My PM doesn't understand why this project is so hard."

"My team doesn't get any of the good projects."

"Our architecture will collapse within six months."

"Carryover is a fact of life on this team."

"We need to replatform to survive peak."

"We're making the right investments to survive peak."

"My tech lead has me over-engineer everything."

A team is a cacophony of stories. You'll hear them at obvious times, like during a project kickoff. You'll hear them as asides in one-on-ones, glossed over without explanation because they're so "obvious" to the teller. You'll hear them as jokes in sprint planning sessions, poking fun at tensions between team members. You'll hear them as people get ready to start a meeting, in standup updates, in email, around the coffee machine. People share stories pretty much whenever they get together.

Stories don't appear fully formed. They emerge as people draw connections between evidence. Imagine a stakeholder with limited visibility into the activities of a team. They might find the work that they request is frequently delayed and then abruptly deprioritized. They might not think much of it the first time. When it becomes a pattern, the stakeholder begins talking about how the team is unreliable and underperforming.

The team's tech lead might tell an entirely different story. They eagerly jump on projects, but have trouble hitting estimates. Over multiple sprint retros, they identify a neglected system that is impeding a range of work streams. Rather than continue to struggle, they decide to pause feature work for a sprint so that they can shore up the neglected system. To the tech lead, this is another great example of how their team learns from problems and strengthens its ability to deliver.

Stories are typically incomplete, but rarely wrong. A story like that stakeholder's can be frustrating to hear as a manager. You likely have a more balanced and nuanced view of your team. Yet others are now acquiring a negative perception of them and becoming less willing to trust them with important work.

Thankfully, as managers, we're uniquely positioned to shape the stories that people tell. Our roles usually ensure that we get face time with a large cross-section of an organization. Use that time to share the evidence that speaks to the breadth of what your team is engaging with. Don't stop there. Connect the dots and draw your audience to the stories that you want them to be telling.

Repetition is an important tool for spreading stories. Call out complementary groupings of evidence. Take every opportunity to retell a story. Maybe you've been impressing upon a team that it should get in control of the operational aspects of its system. Maybe an engineer says in a standup that they fixed a chronic issue after digging into some confusing log messages. Pull this piece of evidence into the broader story you're trying to tell: "I'm glad we're taking the time to get in control of the operational aspects of our system."

It's a good sign when people are nodding along and signaling familiarity with a story. It means the story is no longer background noise. They're consciously using it to assess the world around them. It's a better sign when you hear people repeating stories you tell. It means a story has resonated at a deeper level, that it has become a tool for achieving their goals. People are now tracking to your direction without you having to stand over their shoulders.

When negative stories spread, they give you an opportunity to connect with your audience. Oftentimes, all you need to do is ask. Someone who is telling others that they're frustrated with your team would likely welcome the opportunity to tell you why they're frustrated. Ask questions to understand their evidence. This will help you understand their values. A stakeholder who sees a team as unreliable is telling you what he thinks reliability looks like. He could be telling you how he values the different capabilities of your team, potentially that he doesn't know how to place a value on some of them. He could be telling you where he gets his evidence and how information flows through an organization. These kinds of conversations are opportunities to win over detractors, but you should also be open to changing your mind about a situation. You could find that you're misaligned with an organization's objectives and that you need to retune.

You want to be telling the best stories. Make them stick. Own the narrative.

The Path to Change: Facts and Feelings

Mary Lynn Manns

"They just won't change." How many times have you said this in frustration? If you have, let's think about how you are trying to persuade people.

As an engineer, you pride yourself in being analytical. You can make a solid case with an organized collection of data. But when others don't respond with a desire to change, you might think it's because they just don't under-stand—so you offer more data, more facts, more logic.

However, it's likely that your listeners do understand. They just don't *care* about your data as much as they *care* about something else that is more important to them.

Consider the word "care." What one person cares about is not necessarily what another person cares about. For example, although you are providing data that supports a process change in the organization, others may push back because they care more about the learning curve, the time, and the potential risks along the way. They might be thinking about previous changes they believe are similar—because these didn't work, they worry your idea won't either. Care...believe...worry. You might not see these feelings as rational, but they are strong, influential, and cause people to dig in their heels. None of us are Mr. Spock from *Star Trek*. None of us are totally rational. We make decisions based on information and how we *feel* about that information.

This is why when you're trying to persuade someone to accept a different view, you must consider the beliefs and feelings behind the resistance. When you make your argument with clear and complete data, this is only the first step. The resistor will likely react by pointing out the weaknesses in your argument—many of us are good at this and even enjoy it! Our human ten-dency toward "confirmation bias" makes us more interested in seeking out information that agrees with our own views. How many times have you felt a rush of excitement when you discovered information that supports you? We are not as good at recognizing the holes in our own beliefs because…well, who would enjoy being wrong? In fact, the backfire effect suggests that when you offer information that conflicts with what others believe, it might actually cause them to hold onto their position even more strongly.

So how can we persuade these irrational, emotion-filled humans around us? Help them to *care* about the idea you are presenting. Rather than a collection of bullet points, present information in an inspirational story that allows your listener to *feel* the problem and the proposed solution. Even better, encourage them to write the story—to spark their imagination and *feel* the possibilities. Change happens one person at a time, so make an effort to understand individual needs and concerns. Then, rather than focusing only on how the change will help the organization, build some individual *excitement* by showing how it will address your listeners' interests and pain points. At the same time, recognize the losses that people are *feeling* as a result of the change. And rather than wearing yourself out by trying to convince resistors that won't budge, why not invite them to join the team? This acknowledges that you respect their concerns and, because they see things differently, they can help uncover issues you may be missing.

This is not easy. Data is logical, whereas feelings are messy. But if you haven't been successful with trying to coax everyone to your side with logic, consider the possibility that the path to change is an emotion-filled partnership that should make use of facts as well as feelings, concerns, and curiosities in order to form the best idea possible.

People Leave Bad Managers, Not Bad Jobs —Right?

Nik Knight

You will often hear that people don't leave bad jobs, they leave bad managers. As with many meme-friendly pearls of wisdom, there is far more to it than that; sometimes people do leave because of problems with their boss, but there are a whole host of other factors that push or pull people to a new opportunity.

Before I go further, full disclosure: I've been a manager for around 10 years now, and in that time, a number of direct and indirect reports have left my team. Each one had their reasons for leaving, and I freely admit that for some, I was at least part of that reason. So, this is not a defensive reaction on my part—I haven't always been the manager people have needed or deserved, and I'm not too proud to admit that. It was all part of my development as a leader, and I only hope that I didn't do too much damage to others in the process.

Having said that, there were a good many reasons for people deciding to move on that were beyond my ability to influence. Partners got job offers in other parts of the world. Some people—especially those in the early stages of their careers—worked out that actually, they weren't on the right path for them. Or in the right city. Or earning the right salary. For some, opportunities arose that were just too good to turn down. The greatest line manager in the world would struggle to compete in these scenarios.

Deciding to change jobs is rarely due to a single root cause—what decision ever is, really?—it's often a multidimensional thing, even though there might be a catalyst that finally tips people over from "meh" to "I'm outta here!" This is the space where a good manager can make a difference and pull someone who is wavering back from the edge.

A line manager who is interested in their team members' well-being, checks in frequently, monitors morale, and so on, stands a far better chance of spotting the warning signs of a flight risk, and can therefore choose to address problems early. An opportunity to learn a new skill, a change of project, a tweak to working hours — there's a million things that could make a world of difference to someone struggling to find the joy in their day-to-day routine. Of course, there's nothing to stop any manager from doing this — those who don't aren't necessarily bad managers though, they are just not yet proficient at this skill.

Sometimes, though, even when they have a diligent, caring manager who's totally on top of what their team needs and how to keep them engaged, people still opt to take the path out. This generally points to a bigger problem — the team culture might be healthy, but perhaps the organizational culture is not. I saw a beautifully succinct description of this in a tweet not long ago; "good managers know when to amplify or dampen corporate leadership (*https://oreil.ly/tyIiL*)." I have seen the more talented managers I've encountered do exactly this — but there are limits to how much one person can dampen the effects of a toxic environment. Does this make them a bad manager? Not so much.

So, is there such a thing as a "bad manager" at all? Well, there are certainly people for whom management does not come naturally. For some of these folks, it is a skill they will never quite master, and unfortunately, there are others who don't even see the need to try. There are teams and organizations where developing management and leadership skills just isn't a priority, or where command-and-control is still seen as the standard way to manage. It's not impossible to improve these situations, but it can be exhausting swimming against that tide—there must be the will to change in the mix somewhere.

Do people leave people who are (currently) doing a not-so-great job of management? Hell, yes! Is that the only reason they leave? No. Not by a long shot. The best thing we can do as managers is to regularly take a long, hard, clear-eyed look at ourselves and ask, "Am I being the manager this person, this team needs me to be?" If the answer is yes, great — good for you, keep going. If not, maybe it's time to think about what you could change that would make a real difference to the team you serve.

Performance Is an Ongoing Conversation

Ines Sombra

What can you do when a goal is realistic, conversations are happening, and a person is still not performing as expected in their role? A performance improvement plan (PIP) is not the only course of action. There are many strategies to address performance challenges sooner, and they greatly depend on the cause of the problem—a specific event versus something systemic.

Event-Based Behavior

Events like a breakup, family changes, illness, and more challenge us all and make it difficult to focus on work. It's your responsibility as a leader to create space for life to happen and expect that there might always be something going on in your organization. Here are some things you may want to try in this situation:

- Use your one-on-ones to discuss what is happening in your report's life, provide time off, or explore the possibility of a leave. Remind your report that they can take advantage of the company's counseling resources (if you have this benefit).

- Have a notion of how much the current situation is affecting your direct report's goals so that you can help course correct after things settle down. I like to keep an achievement log for myself and all of my direct reports and use it to frame our discussions. We make sure that we note big wins and accomplishments, and then I compare them to the objectives that I know my report wants to achieve. If there's already enough progress in a specific area, the temporary slowdown is not as impactful.

Ultimately, you might not be able to do much about what's causing diminished performance in this case. But you can weather the storm together and remember where true north is so you can get back there when it passes.

Systemic Behavior

There can be many reasons why underperformance becomes systemic, and the way you address them is very much aligned with the nature of the problem. Here are a few strategies that you might want to try when performance suffers:

- Inability to follow through:
  - Try some lightweight goal setting, training, mentorship, rescoping of work
  - Provide the option of extra program management support (if you have it)
  - Use your one-on-ones to assess together how well different approaches are working and to promptly communicate blockers

- Team dynamics getting in the way:
  - Look at your team processes, current staffing needs, work demands, and so on and make adjustments. For example, if work can't be completed due to code reviews being difficult to come by, have the team prioritize reviews above new work to unblock peers. Or if your code review cycles are too long, you can help the team articulate a shared criteria around good reviews (maybe for this system we care more about stability than code style). A shared language might help your team avoid pedantic arguments that consume too much review time.

- Lack of motivation or when problems have become stale:
  - If possible, add variety to your report's responsibilities, like mentoring junior engineers on the domain they are experts in so that they can take over the tasks that have become so monotonous.
  - You might want to look into resetting job responsibilities to broaden the scope. Have this person assist in areas that are different, or maybe even facilitate a move to a different project.

- Constant exhaustion:
  - Keep an eye out for your team's workload and emergency interventions. A team who has been performing heroics keeping a system up won't be able to sustain regular performance expectations and is well deserving of some rest.
  - Keep track of on-call rotations, incidents, number of alerts firing, and prioritize their remediations. Fixing the root cause of operational exhaustion is paramount.

- Goals being unclear:
  — It's difficult to be enthusiastic about a task that comes out of the blue and seems arbitrary. By clarifying objectives and contextualizing work within business needs, you can help your reports understand why something needs to be done. Sometimes, clarification of the business goal can even result in a more efficient solution with greater team buy-in.

Lastly, there is a special case of systemic behavior from which it is extremely difficult to recover. When a working relationship turns adversarial, it is very rare that things will get better, no matter how much you try. You have my sympathy if you're ever in this spot. It's one of the most difficult and demoralizing times for a leader. Here are some things to explore when performance suffers due to an adversarial relationship with your direct report:

- Reach out to your HR person and ask for guidance.
- Hone in your conflict navigation skills. Attend workshops for having difficult conversations, providing effective feedback, etc.
- Prepare for your one-on-ones; you might even want to have the main points written down to make sure you phrase things well.
- Consider having one-on-ones mediated by someone from HR if things are really bad.
- Don't neglect your self-care, this situation will drain you and very much stress you out.

And, most important, don't put off taking action. When things are not going well set a kind and reasonable resolution time in your mind, try everything you can to improve things, and if things don't get better stick to your decision date. Reach out to HR and explore your company's formal processes for termination. It's very difficult to end a working relationship but you owe it to your team to not put off the decision.

To sum up, many causes can affect an individual's performance. Taking the time to diagnose them allows you to better respond and support your direct reports. Even though some things might be beyond your control, you have the advantage of sharing a common goal: the growth and nurturing of their career.

Physician, Heal Thyself!

Jeff Foster

There's no doubt about it, being an engineering manager can be a stressful role. Responsible for some combination of people, product, process, and the technology, you have many responsibilities, and if you're not careful, it's going to eat you alive. To be effective, you need to learn to manage yourself before you can manage others.

If you come into work feeling under pressure, you are going to transmit this to the rest of your team. If this sounds like pseudo-science, take a look at the research; emotional contagion is a *thing*. Research from Caroline Bartel (*https://oreil.ly/Boygl*) (at New York University) and Richard Saavedra (*https://oreil.ly/l-JR0*) (University of Michigan) has shown that people share moods within hours. As an engineering manager you have the biggest influence in the team; people take their cues from you. You can't lead others when you're in the wrong frame of mind.

So, how do you look after yourself?

First, make sure you work at a sustainable pace. Elon Musk might regularly work 100-hour weeks, but it's not a sustainable way to lead an organization! One of the principles I strongly agree with in the Agile Manifesto is to "promote sustainable development." As an engineering manager you should lead by example by working in a sustainable way. Don't answer emails at 2 a.m. or come in over the weekend, and definitely don't be the first one in and last one out every single day.

Second, look after yourself physically. This doesn't mean running a marathon at 4 a.m. or anything heroic. Start simple; take a walk after lunch, play some sport or maybe go to the gym. Small changes make a huge difference. As Dr Nick Cavill says, "If exercise were a pill, it would be one of the most cost-effective drugs ever invented."

So far, so obvious. My final point is probably the most important but most neglected part of being a manager. Look after yourself mentally.

Mental health is just as important as physical health, but we don't do a good enough job of talking about it openly and honestly, nor do we take note of the real impact it can have on team performance. There's a stigma associated with mental health and it needs to be broken down.

How can you look after yourself mentally?

One key part of this is having regular one-on-ones with your manager. Regular one-on-ones should allow you to talk openly and honestly about the issues affecting you and (much more important!) *how* they are affecting you. This is easier said than done, and you'll need a high degree of psychological safety to do this. Building this degree of trust and openness with your manager will make it much easier for you to do the same thing with your team.

Another option is mindfulness training. If going to the gym works for your body, mindfulness does the same for your brain.

How do you train mindfulness? One simple exercise you can try is just to take five minutes out each day to focus on your breathing. Find a quiet place, close your eyes and focus your attention on your breath. Be as curious as you can—what parts of your body move as you breathe? How is each breath different from your last? Try five minutes like this each day for a month and see whether it makes a difference for you.

When you're confident that you have yourself looked after, help your team members look after themselves. Strive to create a psychologically safe environment in which people can share their feelings without fear of recrimination and you'll set the team up for success.

Physician, heal thyself!

Political Capital and the Favor Economy

Brian Fitzpatrick

Whether you're interested in it or not, politics affect almost every aspect of your career, and when you interact with someone else in your company, you're either gaining or spending political capital.

There are hundreds of ways to gain political capital at work, from shipping product to mentoring a new teammate, to doing code reviews, or even interviewing candidates for your team. Basically, anything that you do at work that your management chain wants done or just sees as valuable will gain you political capital. You can even gain political capital by doing favors for other folks in your company.

Every company has a gray-market *favor economy* that lives off the organization chart, and those favors are one of the things that you can use to fill up your political bank account. There's usually something you can quickly and easily do that benefits your company but is someone else's job that would take them much, much longer to perform (if they can even do it at all). If you keep your eyes open for the chance to do these things (or if someone comes right out and asks you to do something for them), you earn a bit of credit for your bank account in this favor economy. And the size of this credit is directly proportional to the difficulty that the other person would have had performing this task: if it takes you five minutes but would have taken them a full day, you get a "day's" credit in the eyes of the other person.

Think of these credits as a series of small bets: some will never pay you back, others will pay even money, and still others will pay enormous dividends. It's difficult to know which bets will pay off, and, of course, if someone is trying to take advantage of you, it's best not to play! But one thing that will pay off over time is that people will remember you as the person who helped them out in a jam. Later on, when you're in a jam and you give them a call, they're going to be considerably more likely—even eager—to help you out than if you gave them a big, fat "not my job" response when they came looking for help. Even if you never get "paid back" you'll often learn something new in the process of helping someone, and it simply feels good to help other people, so what do you have to lose other than a little time and effort?

Conversely, every time you need to plead your case for something or go up against someone else in your company, you're *spending* political capital. If you spend all your capital winning a bunch of battles that don't matter, you're going to find that you have nothing left in your account when it comes to the important things. Be strategic and fight for things either that matter or that you're pretty sure you have some chance of winning. Blowing all your capital on a battle that you know you can't win is pointless, stressful, and career limiting for no good reason.

Most industries (especially the tech industry!) are a lot smaller than you think, and people talk more than you think, so the person you stick it to today might very well be the one who kills your job application 10 years from now. So, unless you're planning to move to a desert island, burning bridges will almost always be a costly mistake. Friends come and go, but enemies accumulate.

You'll tap this same political bank account when you need to ask a favor of someone else in your company. It might be that you need someone to do something for you, or you do something that steps on someone else's toes, or you even just disagree with someone else in your company. It's incredibly useful to develop an awareness of when you're gaining political capital, and when you're spending it. If you fail to develop this awareness, there's a good chance that your account will be drained before you know it, leaving you powerless in your organization (and your career).

One of the most interesting things about political capital and the favor economy is that your bank account doesn't just empty out when you leave a job or a company—you'll frequently be able to call on folks at your company for a hand even after you've left. This is all the more reason that you should never burn bridges when you leave a company, no matter how tempting it might seem at the time.

Prioritize Building Relationships with Your Peers

Rocio Delgado

When we become managers, we become responsible for the success of the team that we are leading. We immediately start building relationships with our direct reports, managing career development, removing blockers, providing context, helping set goals and resolving conflicts. We begin spending time in one-on-ones on a recurrent basis to get to know them, understand their drivers, and help them to grow and achieve their goals.

Although all of this is extremely important, it's critical to build similar relationships with your peers across the organization. Neglecting to do so contributes to the creation of silos, poor decision making, and potentially an "us versus them mentality," which causes collaboration problems between teams.

As managers, our peers are our team #1 and not our direct reports.

Team #1, as described by Patrick Lencioni, in his book *Five Dysfunctions of a Team*, refers to the team that is your priority. When a leader makes the team they're directly managing the priority over everything else, it's easy to forget that they are part of the larger organization and that they need alignment with peer teams to make sure they are working toward the proper set of goals.

To be part of a cohesive organization, everyone should pay attention to the collective set of goals and results above the individual interest of the team they manage. This might sound counterintuitive or even feel disloyal, but think about it as an orchestra. If musicians of the string sections work in isolation from the percussion section, the music is not going to come out as it should, even if each musician is the best at what they do.

Executive teams often apply this concept; however, it's applicable at any level. Whether you work in a product engineering team, infrastructure, SRE, or QA, you need to build relationships with the group of leaders with whom you collaborate. Together you will define priorities, schedule releases, develop a strategy for your products, and so on, and this collaboration is critical to your success and in consequence the success of the team or organization that you are responsible for.

That is why it is also essential to prioritize spending time with your peers the same way you do with your direct reports.

How Do You Do That?

Here are some steps to follow:

- Identify your first team. This is everyone with whom you collaborate to make collective decisions for the team and the organization.
- In addition to planning and other project-related meetings, spend time with your peers in one-on-ones on a recurring basis. This may not be as frequent as with your direct reports, but this will provide you with the required context to understand their perspective when it comes time to make decisions. More important, this is your time to build trust with them.
- Establish how you want to work together. Communicate clearly what you are responsible for, and identify the areas that may overlap.
- Define how you want to make cross-group decisions and establish the individual and collective goals.
- Check those goals periodically.
- Communicate how you want to receive feedback and ask how they want to receive feedback.
- Share what you are learning, concerns, and any context that might be helpful to them.

Spending time with your peers across the organization will provide everyone with context and information to make better decisions. This prevents the creation of silos, and fosters the ability to be emphatic when disagreements occur, all leading to a better decision-making process.

Priority Exceptions

Beau Lebens

Constantly changing priorities and surprise projects erode team morale and leave everyone unsure of whether they're working on the most important thing, or whether they'll ever get to finish anything. Even though being adaptable and flexible is critical for most teams, it's always important to have some kind of roadmap and approach to prioritization and planning work. There are many different ways to plan and prioritize your work; what's important is that when priorities change—and they will change—you acknowledge that change and adapt quickly.

If you don't clearly acknowledge the change in plans, your team can start to question the point of the plan in the first place. They'll begin to wonder whether they are expected to do this new thing *and* the old thing, or just the new thing, or because the new thing is not in the plan, perhaps the team should actually ignore it? Don't leave room for interpretation. Clearly set expectations and make sure you communicate unambiguously what is being asked of them. Sometimes, your team needs to be given clear "permission" to really work on this new thing, and delay or drop the old thing.

On my teams, we use a process we call a *Priority Exception* to clearly address a major change in our plans. This process is used when we had a plan of work, and for some reason something not on that plan jumps to the next most important thing for us to work on. The goal is to acknowledge the change, clearly communicate the impact this change will have on existing work, and critically, highlight why it is so important that it should disrupt our plan. We use this template to ensure the right information is always included, and we distribute the details to everyone on the team (and any other relevant stakeholders).

What New Thing Is Happening?

Right at the outset, we outline the new work at a high level so that we all know what we're talking about. We link out to our project management system or code tracker for further details. This section includes which individuals or teams will be required for the new work.

What Existing Thing Is Being Delayed?

Next, we specify what work we're putting on hold or slowing down because of this new work, or how we're creating capacity to work on it. We try to include details on the expected impact of our delay; If we can put a number on it, this is where it goes. Lost revenue? Delayed launch? Losing more users? Be specific.

Why Is the New Thing More Important?

This helps head off questions about why we had to "drop everything" to work on something unexpected. This should clearly demonstrate why the new work is more important or more urgent than the planned work. You should be able to clearly illustrate why it offsets the impact of the delayed work (as previously detailed).

How Did This Come About?

As a form of mini-retrospective, this is a chance to highlight why this work was such a surprise. It's an opportunity to learn and avoid surprises in the future, or come up with other mitigation strategies, depending on what happened.

Timeline

We set a clear timeline covering any wind-down of current work, transition to the new work, and expected completion or progress milestones. Because Priority Exceptions often come with an external deadline, we make sure that is clearly communicated, as well.

Priority Exceptions are a useful, lightweight tool for communicating changes in priorities, and for learning how to reduce priority-thrash over time. Teams have appreciated the clarity that Priority Exceptions bring to otherwise potentially confusing times, and the clear permission they give to delay work in favor of something more important.

The Product Manager's Concerns

Travis Donia

As an engineering leader, you can improve the quality of the product you deliver by helping your team interface effectively with product managers (PMs). To do this it helps to open a dialog with the PM about their requests. Here are some common concerns they have and ways to open up a conversation about them.

Users

A core responsibility of the PM is to know what's important to the user, so it's normal for them to come to you excited at having just learned something about the users. They want to reflect that feedback in the product. As a manager, it's helpful for you to dig into why they're excited so that you can transmit it to your team. Understanding where the feedback came from and how they intend to make your users' lives better will also help you to make sure the implementation delivers the impact the PM is excited about.

Money

What a feature will cost and how much revenue potential it has are the basis for forecasting the return a PM will get from an investment of your team's attention. The expected return on investment (ROI) is one of the most basic ways a product manager can prioritize. Often, this is expressed in terms of *effort*. Asking, "How much effort is X versus Y versus Z and what will I get out of them?" can be a proxy for, "I want all three, but I know I have to fit inside a budget and hit a target." In these situations, you can help them understand the trade-offs and, in turn, gain a better understanding of their priorities.

Time

Like money, time is also a finite resource that the PM will need to budget. Time has an added wrinkle because it's not fungible, so getting something shipped before a deadline can hold significant value. For instance, if there's a big marketing spend that's been scheduled, the PM will probably have specific features that need to be shipped beforehand. When in doubt, ask what's driving a deadline so that you can align your team's schedule with the product's.

Just because the timing of an ask is flexible when it's first mentioned, it might not remain so. If it sits in the backlog for too long, it will eventually sprout a deadline. When that happens too frequently, a defensive mode many organizations fall into is to assume everything must be scheduled before it's requested. This takes away your ability to plan your team's time, which is ultimately less efficient for everyone.

Impact

What is the effect that a PM hopes to achieve? For a nascent product, driving sign-ups might be the highest impact activity at the beginning. For a more mature product, impact can come from changes to users' patterns of behavior within your product. To understand how the PM is thinking about impact, open a conversation about the metrics that a PM is watching and the key use cases they hope your product will serve.

Other features are more obligatory: a password reset page might not move the needle, but is critical to the product's existence. It can be more difficult to motivate your team to build these features, but it will help if you and they understand the rationale behind them.

Bugs

Bugs happen, and are often laden with tension. Both the PM and your team will feel frustrated by a setback: PMs hate having their budgets drained with an unexpected expense, and your team will likely feel that someone, somewhere, messed up and they're being blamed for it. In the moment, your ability to focus everyone on a constructive response rather than blame is critical to getting the team fully engaged in fixing it.

Longer term, work with both PMs and your team to establish a culture that understands how blameless debugging will help you solve bugs faster. That tendency will also make your team more likely to spot issues before they ship. You can also help the PM understand the trade-offs early in the planning process so that they're aware of the technical debt and risk it creates. Sometimes, they'll choose to pay down that debt and will look to you to guide that investment. Finally, accept as inevitable that some bugs will happen. In many businesses, software that ships without bugs has probably taken too long to build; as a manager, it's your job to work with the PM to find the balance between speed and correctness that's appropriate for your product.

Obviously, there's no one-size-fits-all way of understanding every request you'll receive, but as a manager, there's value in your opening the conversation up with PMs. By learning to talk with the product leaders about their requests, you'll gain a deeper understanding of what they're trying to accomplish. A good PM will use the same conversations to learn your language as well. Over time, the requests you receive will be easier to understand because you'll share more context. Ultimately, the product you ship will reflect the quality of that conversation.

Thank you to Stephanie Wai for reading and editing drafts of this essay.

Projects for Which Agile Is Inappropriate

Ron Lichty

I encountered Agile for the first time in 1999. Ten years later, I was not only coaching my own teams in it but also teaching it to friends' teams. One of the questions I repeatedly heard in those days was, "Is Agile appropriate for every kind of software project?"

I wracked my brain for some possible kind of software development for which Agile wouldn't be a fit. I didn't have a good response.

The answer leapt out at me a few years later. It was staring me in the face. I'd been stymied because I was looking for a kind of software. The answer was instead a kind of environment. Micromanagement. Agile is not a fit for command-and-control environments.

Micromanagement disrupts Agile. Micromanagement prevents best teams. Micromanagement prevents learning. Micromanaged teams become order takers.

Agile's self-organizing teams call for everyone on the team to step up. Micromanagement causes everyone to step back.

For teams to self-organize, they must be nurtured, not thwarted. For most teams, self-organization holds the promise to be the most powerful part of Agile—and possibly the most fragile. Over the course of two decades introducing Agile into my teams and more recently parachuting into organizations purportedly already Agile, I've repeatedly run into organizations signed up for the ceremonies and practices—sprints, standups, planning, points, backlogs, frequent delivery and the rest—without ever embracing the values and mindset behind them. That is, I've repeatedly run into organizations that need to let go of "telling" and embrace "teaming."

Ask any group of product people who've been at it for a while to think back to their best team ever, and they'll never describe a team that was micromanaged. Instead, when asked to describe that "best team," they'll come up with characteristics like "respect" and "trust" and "shared purpose" and "we had each other's backs." They'll also, in a nanosecond, sign up to be on a team like that again.

In its Aristotle Study of what distinguishes its high-performance teams, Google identified a singular standout, defining characteristic, "psychological safety." The study further described psychological safety as everyone at the table feeling welcome to speak up, each team member speaking about equally, and each feeling listened to. It could be identified visually by "equality in distribution of conversational turn-taking."

In his eye-opening best seller *Drive: The Surprising Truth about What Motivates Us*, Daniel Pink calls out autonomy as a key to intrinsically motivating people and teams. "Intrinsically motivated people usually achieve more than their reward-seeking counter-parts," Pink notes.

Agile gives those of us who are managers the role of "servant leaders." In its manifesto, Agile calls out building projects around motivated individuals, trusting to get the job done, face-to-face conversation, and self-organizing teams—teams that reflect and tune and adjust.

Servant leadership means we managers are not the directors but the facilitators and enablers. We're looking to create cultures in which teamwork and psychological safety and autonomy thrive—in which *everyone* in our organizations, right down to the interns, are leaders, each one of us leading from our unique expertise and experience. Make no mistake, few interns are leading software architecture—but our interns likely do have insights from their boilerpot of sometimes edgy schoolwork that's worth listening to and learning from. (And if they don't, we probably hired the wrong interns!)

Agile practices are useful. They're designed to support great teams. Even in the context of micromanagement, Agile practices can make a difference; but in micromanaged environments, their benefit is limited.

It's incumbent upon us managers to support Agile practices by crafting the culture and the environment for great teams to emerge and thrive, not by telling teams what to do but by setting objectives and boundaries and then turning our focus to *nurturing* teams to deliver their best.

Only by avoiding telling and by nurturing teaming do we offer our organizations the possibility to deliver their best.

Reconciliation Loops

Kevin Stewart

In distributed systems, there has been a continual push to make systems *self-healing*. We can find one implementation of this in Kubernetes. Kubernetes is based on the concept of a declarative specification of the *desired state* of the cluster and the use of *reconciliation loops* to drive the actual state toward the desired state.

In a Kubernetes cluster, there are several components that work together to implement this behavior. The primary component is the *pod*, which has one or more *containers*, and is the unit that gets scheduled onto a *node* in the cluster. Containers reside in an *image registry*, and when placed on a node are governed by the container runtime on that node and a process known as a *kubelet*.

One node in the cluster is considered the master node where all the control-plane components reside. The *API server* handles incoming requests and updates the etcd database with state changes. The *scheduler* is responsible for determining which nodes are appropriate to allocate a given workload. Finally, the *controller* manager coordinates a set of controllers that make up the reconciliation loops that drive the entire cluster to the desired state.

In a properly managed Kubernetes cluster, this system works fairly well. There is mostly a clear separation of duties and loose coupling. Although there is some initial pain in getting this all set up, after it's operational and tuned, Kubernetes can provide a solid, self-healing environment for applications.

So, what does this have to do with engineering leadership? The concept of reconciliation loops maps pretty close to the (often unintentional) behavior seen in many organizations. Let's look at one way in which entities in Kubernetes might map to organizational constructs:

- Cluster: organization
- Container: person
- Pod: team
- Node: department
- Scheduler: vice president
- Controller Manager: department head
- Controller: manager
- Kubelet: program/product/project manager
- Image Registry: the pipeline

Most organizations desire some degree of self-healing. Business conditions are constantly changing, and the organization needs to adapt to the current conditions. From the outside, it looks like all of the components of the cluster are in place and operational, yet the organization is not reaching its desired state.

Is your organization a "mirror-tocracy"? Inspect your pod specifications and look at what images you're pulling and from which registries, Are you defaulting to Apache and MySQL when NGINX and PostgreSQL might be better for your use case? Are you using those components because that's what's familiar? To translate: are your teams really made up of the right people with the right skills for what you are trying to accomplish?

Diversifying your container images is a good first step, but much more is needed to make a shift stick. That's where it pays to pay attention to the reconciliation loops. Does your scheduler have a certain node affinity bias? (Does leadership tend to focus mostly on only one or two of your teams?) Are your controllers implementing inefficient algorithms that, in conjunction with the controller manager, get you close to the desired state but never all the way there? (Are your managers failing to deliver?) Perhaps it's time to rewrite or replace those controllers, perhaps it's time to restructure the management chain.

Systems thinking is not limited to software. Advancements can be made by looking at a variety of systems and applying lessons learned from them. One should not blindly apply solutions they find from other systems thinking that will solve their issues. Instead, look at these systems for inspiration because they can lead you to more creative solutions.

"Remote"

Silvia Botros

I never liked that term "remote." It is exclusionary. And betrays a sense of "otherness" that I feel is unhealthy for team cohesion. I understand that not everyone finds it easy or productive to work mostly apart from daily, in-person, social interaction. But success is an arm-in-arm effort, and the strategies to build successful teams work regardless of geography if we reward the appropriate behaviors.

I work remotely and have been for a few years since a couple of family moves. It has been a mostly successful experience this time around. What I do not talk about often is the story of when I didn't succeed as a remote employee, resulting in being laid off years ago. And I think it's important to talk about that, as well. Because as gratifying as it might be to claim full credit at my current success, I'd be dishonest to pretend that success was all me.

So, what is it that makes the same person excel or fail miserably at the same thing? Let me share some of my experience around this and how I think it might matter to your organization.

The Team

There is never a "successful remote employee." There is always a "team that communicates well" and this goes beyond locality and who's physically where. I've seen engineering teams in the same office fail spectacularly at basic communication around work in progress or around setting expectations for delivering feature work, whereas other teams spanning three different time zones efficiently produce results. This is all a roundabout way for me to say that my success is really my team's success. There are a number of habits that make my team so good at this and they are worth calling out:

- Most conversations happen in chat, keeping everyone in the loop.
- Joining standups from laptops, even for those in the office. Everyone is on the same communication channels.

- In meetings where a large portion of the group is in a big room, someone is designated as representative of those calling in. That way we can still get the group's attention and ask questions if we want to.

These are not just behaviors that are useful when the entire team isn't local. Life happens, coworkers have to work from home sometimes, errands, all sorts of things. Allowing for your people to still be part of important discussions while living life is a real sign of wanting life balance for your people and not just talking about it.

The Effects of Human Laziness

Humans are by nature lazy: we do not seek what we do not see. And we make presumptions about things we do not know for a fact. These natural shortcuts our brains take will always show themselves in the systems we design. I have seen it multiple times where teams have developed and deployed software that did not actually meet all the needs of the business only for retrospectives later to declare the "root cause" a failure in communication.

It amazes me how often organizations will over and over again prove Conway's law in this specific dynamic. Teams that communicate only to humans in front of them will also fail to involve all stakeholders in decisions in design, will fail to notify other teams when they are about to ratchet up customer involvement in their new beta, and will create products that ultimately are a reflection of how the team itself handles its communication. It has been my experience that teams that put the effort into being good at communication, at writing things down, and at making everything explicit, also find the most alignment and find all their members rowing in the same direction. Having people work from wherever they live at this point becomes the cherry on top.

Hiring, Diversity, and Inclusion

Here's a harsh truth: if you require hiring in a specific geographic location but pinky swear that you value diversity and inclusion, you are at best misguided as to how to create diverse teams and how to keep underrepresented groups included. Intent doesn't matter when hiring practices have the opposite impact.

If you decide to open the experienced roles to "anywhere US" but none of your engineering managers have previously managed people not local to them or, worse, are not interested in that, you are hiring experienced engineers to see them fail.

We are in an industry that has far more demand for talent than is available to hire. And that's an advantage for us as workers. I see companies clearly state hiring as a challenge and something that's a competitive edge, yet they hamstring those same efforts by requiring that people relocate. Not only does this make hiring more difficult, but it is also not inclusive.

Risk Budgets: Five Choices Between Your Team and Failure

Cris Concepcion

In modern software development, we prize innovation, and by association, we also reward risk taking. "Move fast and break things" and "Fail fast, fail often" are mottos that have defined our industry. Although it might be worth taking our time to do a good job, often, knowing what a good job looks like requires guessing on imperfect information and adjusting course. We need to take risks if it can lead to discovery.

However, it's also easy for us to be blinded by this bias toward action and to break things that destroy customer trust or to let pervasive ambiguity displace future clarity. As engineering managers, making these strategic trade-offs between risk and caution is a constant part of our job.

Suppose that your team is starting a new feature with an opportunity to play with an exciting new framework that's all the rage everywhere. You have some product owners who are eager to get started, especially because this is new for everyone, and there are some theories that they want to explore. As you discuss the roadmap with them, you begin to realize that your team's going to be iterating on this project for a while.

Already, you're taking on three small risks:

- Your team is working with unfamiliar tools
- Product owners don't have a scope locked down yet
- The timeline for the project is open ended

Should you reject the project? Likely not yet. These risks feel manageable, and beyond them are exciting opportunities, but three months later, you might be mired by tools that don't live up to the hype, with a product team that hasn't found their direction yet, and developers demoralized by having no end in sight. And you'll ask yourself: how did we get here?

Outside of work, I sometimes like to go rock climbing, occasionally outdoors. There's a certain affinity between climbers and software developers. A climbing route is as much a mental puzzle as it is a physical challenge, and outdoor climbers also exist in this liminal space of pervasive risk. Climbers work with multiple redundant safety systems, so when catastrophic failures happen, it's a result of several insignificant risks that compound on one another.

Near the end of a successful day, a climbing team feels like taking one last challenge. It's late, the light is fading, and so the climber and their partner hurry themselves to finish. They breeze through checking their anchors, which have been reliable all day, and begin climbing in earnest. At a hard crux, the climber misses a hold, one of their worn-out anchors breaks and they injure themselves in a fall. Was the mistake going for a hard route? Climbing at the end of the day? Less than thorough inspections? Making that difficult move? Each of these choices, by themselves, are small and normal, but they all built toward the injury.

The idea of risk budgets was synthesized for me by my friend Geoff, who once said to me, "You're five decisions away from getting yourself killed, and the first decision that you made is to go rock climbing." Sometimes the choices compound like this:

Choose to proceed with a task

1. that can fail
2. and has a nontrivial demand on your skill
3. with suboptimal timing, schedule, or urgency
4. and you made a safety assumption that surprised you with being wrong
5. and given all of the risks assumed, a mistake made here is perilous.

The risks can vary, but by writing them out in this way, we now have a budget and can see that taking three small risks feels manageable, but a fourth risk can bring us to the edge of failure. If a fourth choice is necessary, which of our earlier compromises can be mitigated or resolved? If they can't, should we proceed when we can't accommodate any more setbacks?

Your risk budget is a tool to help you thrive in the middle ground between performance and failure and is a counterbalance to sunk cost fallacies. It also isn't a permission slip to make two or three dumb choices. It's up to you to decide what is a risk and what isn't and what is just a bad choice, but for scenarios in which you're seeing small risks metastasize into big problems, this is a framework to catalog the choices you've made and consider whether you can continue or reconsider.

Safety First!

Lisa van Gelder

My top team-debugging tip: if a team is acting in a way that you don't understand, there's probably something making them feel unsafe.

A couple of years ago, I was brought in to debug a team that was going slower and slower. Velocity was going down sprint over sprint, engineers were coming in late, leaving early, and there were times when nobody knew where any of the engineers were, and they weren't answering Slack or email. I was asked if there was something wrong with the engineers; they didn't seem to care about the work. The CEO asked me to evaluate the team and decide whether we should replace them with a more committed team.

I started to debug the team. I paired with the engineers, I went to their ceremonies like sprint planning, standup, retrospectives, and I did one-on-ones with all of the engineers.

I realized something interesting was happening at sprint planning. The Scrum master told me that previously engineers hadn't been finishing their work at the end of the sprint, so he had decided to hold them accountable for getting their work done. He decided to track individual engineer velocity, not team velocity. At sprint planning, each engineer was asked to commit to the stories they would personally complete by the end of the sprint. If they didn't complete any of their stories by the end of the sprint, they had to justify why in front of the entire team and their manager.

The engineers hated this! They told me they felt blamed. Often, they couldn't complete stories because of dependencies on other people or teams, but that didn't matter, they were asked why they hadn't tried harder to resolve the blockers. So, the engineers began to pad their estimates. Velocity went down because they committed to only the stories they *knew* they could get done by the end of the sprint. Sprints ran Monday to Friday. By Thursday most engineers had finished their work but they didn't want to tell that to the PM or the Scrum master because they were afraid that they'd be assigned a story they couldn't finish. So, by Thursday afternoon most of them were hiding around the building and not answering email or slack.

I resolved the velocity problems in two ways: we ended the tracking of individual velocity and individuals committing to work at sprint planning (commitments were shared by the entire team, with no consequence for not completing them) and we broke epics into smaller stories so that there was more chance of completing them by the end of the sprint.

Not only did our velocity triple, but there was also another great side effect of not tracking individual velocity: when engineers were only accountable for getting their own stories done, there was no incentive for senior engineers to coach or mentor juniors—they might not finish their work and get penalized. After we ended the tracking of individual velocity, seniors paired with juniors and coached them, and the overall team was stronger.

Moral of the story: shame is hugely motivational but usually in the opposite way you want.

Scale Communication Through Writing

Saul Diez-Guerra

One of the most difficult challenges in scaling any sort of large human endeavor is effective written communication; other than pushing the limits of technology, there isn't any challenge more troublesome and pricklier.

The complexity of our team's interactions grows exponentially with the number of teammates, in a perverse application of the network effect. As soon as we are lucky enough to hire and grow our team beyond a handful of people, misunderstandings and conflict invariably appear. Most problems in the workplace can be boiled down to interpersonal problems, and the only way out of them, or at least around them, is effective communication.

To make matters worse, the modern team demands that people work together with colleagues on different schedules, in different buildings, time zones, and even cultures and countries. As your organization grows, it silently drifts into meeting madness and—if you are lucky—its communication patterns turn asynchronous. Left unchecked, these patterns end up taking all sorts of shapes and forms: from the management consulting habit of turning everything into an informational slide deck, to protracted email chains sent to questionable *listservs,* or *laissez-faire* internal wikis that become the Wild Wild West.

After you declare meeting bankruptcy and decide that you don't want to let the communication jungle continue to grow unchecked, the work begins by having everyone involved pause and actively acknowledge the shape of the beast: human, asynchronous, written communication is difficult.

A great degree of human communication is nonverbal, be it body language, intonation, or even just the use of silence. There's conflicting scientific literature as to what the extent is of the nonverbal importance, but percentages aside we can all likely agree that it is intuitively important because we all have experienced its absence at times.

To draw a pithy analogy, our favorite music is often made up of words, song, and dance, but when writing to our colleagues we can only count on our words alone, and oftentimes we won't reach the lyrical abilities of our favorite artist (or their songwriter).

With that in mind, everyone needs to put extraordinary care in their writing. As a group, you should foster a culture of appreciation for great writing by celebrating and encouraging it as well as providing resources for everyone to learn. This all takes effort, but it's effort that pays off: great writing compels great thinking, and mindful communication prevents haste and waste.

Alas, writing well is challenging to master and difficult to keep up: effective prose takes time and effort. Buying the team the time to focus on writing by demanding memos to be written and shared ahead of time, by prioritizing written addresses to the company from leadership or instituting periodic, and public updates from every department slowly breeds a culture that values and cares about the written word.

And although we get everyone to focus on their writing, it is key to deploy the appropriate technical tools to store and share everyone's output, and to establish best practices around using them. Given how much energy goes into every piece, try to focus on persistent venues, such as intranet posts or internal wikis, over ephemeral means such as email or Slack. You will also get more mileage out of your words if you share them with entire groups of people (say, a company-wide Google Doc memo) instead of individuals (a Slack PM or an email to an individual who will indubitably archive your words in days, if not hours or minutes).

In short, prioritizing public and persistent outlets over private and ephemeral will not only get every writer a much larger bang for their buck, but it will also advance the communication cause and the written word culture across the team.

Scaling Management by Giving Up Control

Ned Rockson

Every great engineer turned manager discovers they've donned a set of bulky but powerful gloves. These gloves allow them to move much bigger rocks than before but hinder their ability to tinker with the fine details. They will struggle wearing these new gloves because until now they enjoyed and excelled at dealing with fine details. To succeed, the great engineer turned manager must remove themselves from critical design and implementation paths. In this way they empower their team to succeed.

Often the first hurdle comes during the software design process. In the past, this time afforded creativity and abstract problem solving. In the past the engineer turned manager could think out loud, be self-deprecating, and verbally spar with others on their team. In the past, the team had a level of equality.

Now, the engineer turned manager finds their voice has weight. Now, whenever they present a contrary viewpoint, the team quickly finds the truth in this individual's logic. Now, when engineer turned manager thinks out loud, their team takes their words as directives. Now, instead of laughing and bonding with the person, the self-deprecating jokes prompt pity and discomfort from the team. Now, instead of equality between them there exists a power dynamic.

The leadership has endowed the engineer turned manager with a responsibility to drive the business. They must sometimes make the difficult choice to take on technical debt in order to meet a deadline, or choose the simple and boring solution over the new to reduce risk. They must sometimes kill in-progress projects, even when they know it will sadden the team.

The engineer turned manager must view their team's projects as a portfolio. Some projects succeed, whereas others fail. Some projects are hacked together, whereas others are crafted beautifully. Some projects are halted before they see the light of day.

A great engineer makes a great manager because they can apply problem solving to their portfolio. They can understand the business objectives and work backward to how their projects will drive them. Engineers turned managers can understand the vast number of variables involved with timelines. They can understand that most problems do not have a right answer, only one that predicts the best outcomes given all current data. They can do all of this while explaining to their team why and how they make their choices.

If this person instead chooses to solve all of their portfolio's problems themselves, they will fail. Their abilities will not scale because they have limited brain power and an unlimited number of problems to solve. The abilities of the engineer turned manager will serve them worse than the sum of their team's abilities; the team will see their manager as capable and opt to not take the initiative the manager needs them to. Their abilities, although strong, will not help the team grow, and the team will stop desiring to succeed and eventually leave.

But instead of stumbling on this hurdle, a great engineer turned manager can use those powerful gloves to move mountains. They can use the gloves to answer the call from leadership and push the business forward. They can use the gloves to empower their team, punching through obstacles and orchestrating the team and helping them achieve its results.

Six Tips for a New Manager

Akash Bhalla

It's been an interesting transition moving from the role of an individual contributor to that of someone who helps look after a team of people. Here are some of the things I've learned along the way.

1. Be a Zero

In the book *An Astronaut's Guide to Life on Earth*, Chris Hadfield talks about the concept of how in any situation you can be either a "minus one," a "zero," or a "plus one."

As a new manager joining a team, there will be an innate desire to try to prove yourself as immediately productive. This is often echoed as *conventional wisdom* because you try your hardest to be a +1 and make your presence felt.

However, the reality is that most of the time you won't have enough context of a new situation to be a positive influence, and despite your best intentions you end up being a net negative.

So, be a zero.

Listen and understand before you try to change something.

2. Learn to Say "Yes"

When I think back over some of the managers I've worked for, they've often carried an air of hurriedness around them, which created an invisible barrier. As time went on, I went to these types of managers less and less, and the gap between us widened.

As a direct result, I've made a conscious effort to always respond with a "yes" whenever someone asks for a minute of my time. Try your best to remove any conscious or unconscious barriers that you might be creating.

Caveat: This has a potential for being overwhelming, especially when it leads to uncontrollable context switching. If this is the case, replace "yes" with "yes, how about at {later that day}?"

3. Learn to Say "No"

There's a limit to how much any one person can do: trying to put more water into a full bucket isn't going to net you any more water than you already had.

It's tough, but you need to learn to say "no." Understand what the most effective use of your time is, prioritize your demands and then learn to say no to those whose issues don't make the cut, and don't forget to delegate. The alternative won't magically achieve these tasks, and ultimately damages your health, your team and your reputation.

4. Have One-on-Ones

Your most powerful tool as a manager is information; without it, you're screwed. Here's a brief set of tips for your one-on-ones:

- Schedule for at least 30 minutes every week or fortnight.
- Don't have anything immediately after, leave time for it to expand if needed.
- Don't have more than two or three in any one day; they can be mentally exhausting, and you're no use if you can't give your full attention.
- Don't use it as status update, focus on wider questions.
- You shouldn't be doing most of the talking.
- Keep it free form, but have some basic questions and points that you bring up.

5. Stay (Relatively) Technical

Your technical abilities and experience are a big part of what makes you an effective engineering manager. Keeping close to the code is essential to understand the context and to have relevant conversations. If you're anything like me, it's also essential for your own sanity!

However, it's also easy to fall into the trap of doing what's comfortable and familiar rather than what is actually needed. It can feel extremely satisfying and comforting making use of old skills. But there is an entire team of developers there who could do this job as good as, if not better than, you. There might be no other managers, though, and with no one else doing that part of the job, people will begin to suffer due to neglect.

You've made a choice to move your career toward management, which means making a sacrifice. Even though it's essential to stay technical, this is not the same as progressing as an individual contributor or becoming a technical lead. You're there to support.

6. Let Go

One of the most important lessons to learn as a new manager is that you can't do it all, but this is a very difficult lesson to learn. If you're anything like me, the only way to learn this lesson is the hard way.

It can be an extremely difficult transition, going from being a high performer and seeing immediate and tangible results of your work to being an inexperienced manager. You'll become stressed, you'll fall back into old patterns, and you'll question yourself.

Don't expect to avoid this trap; instead, do the following:

- Accept that you'll make this mistake
- Have the knowledge and awareness to try to recognize it when it happens
- Work on recovering when it does

You need to change the ways in which you perceive success. Shift the focus away from your individual contributions and instead measure yourself on the health of your team and their progress as a unit.

Stop Your Team from Bikeshedding, and Saying "Bikeshedding"

Ian Nowland

The term "bikeshedding" has achieved wide usage as a way of calling out nonproductive feedback. The challenge is that the usual situations in which the term is used have ambiguity about which party is at fault. Thus, as a manager, when you hear members of your team dismiss feedback as bikeshedding, it is your responsibility to dig in and ensure that they have sought out the other parties' perspectives and communicated their reasoning. On the flipside, when your team is being accused, take it as a guide that they need to try and raise the quality of their feedback.

For those unfamiliar with the term, the best description is the email that popularized it, from Poul-Henning Kamp to a FreeBSD email list, posted at *http://bikeshed.com/*. What he describes is this process around a decision being critiqued:

1. Experts think deeply about all options and trade-offs and put forward a proposal.

2. The proposal is reviewed by a committee of non-experts.

3. Rather than focus on the deep trade-offs, the committee spends its time voicing objections and making counterproposals only on trivial details.

This is now called bikeshedding. Within companies, the "experts" are individuals or teams that have made a decision. The "committee" comprises stakeholders who don't agree. Their bikeshedding generally takes two forms, either focusing on trivial details of the implementation that don't meet their needs or proposing a completely different solution: "why can't you just do X, instead."

Everyone bikesheds occasionally, for the reasons that we like to have our opinions heard, but do not have time to gain expert knowledge in every area that affects us. In this original formulation, it seems clear the problem is always with the bikeshedders. They are the ones making low-value noise, and so need to hold themselves to a high standard of feedback that has high utility in giving the experts reason to reconsider their decision. Therefore, it seems fine to call out their behavior when they don't.

The flip side of this is that we all see decisions being made by other parties that not only affect us, but some or all of the following are also true:

- We were not consulted as stakeholders in the decision
- The decision does not seem deeply considered
- The decision and its rationale were not communicated well, or at all

So, when we call out details of how they affect us and are told that we are bikeshedding, it is pretty frustrating to not only be heard, but to be dismissed. Now maybe what we are asking is totally wrong, but that gets to the core challenge in this situation: how much work and time should everybody be putting into decisions to make sure all stakeholders are heard, to deeply consider all possibilities and their trade-offs, and to communicate that rationale to all stakeholders in a way that they can understand on their terms? Obviously, that is an impossible standard to hold for all decisions—organizations would never get anything done. What it comes down to, then, is this is really a debate about how much time and stakeholder communication needs to go into making a decision, which is context dependent.

That's what the conversation needs to be about. How do you do that, though?

When your team is accusing others of bikeshedding
Coach them that when making decisions, we need to do a better job of engaging as many stakeholders as we can, ideally getting their alignment, but at minimum communicating what we are doing and why. When we don't do this, and later have stakeholders complaining, we need to understand that even when their complaints are not well founded, the fact that they are complaining means that we have missed. So be patient, explain our reasons, and maybe think about how we want to change our process for similar decisions in the future.

When your team is being called bikeshedders
Coach them to give the experts the benefit of the doubt that they have considered our preferred solution. Especially remember the engineering

adage: "bring requirements not solutions." And like all good behaviors, this applies when we think the expert team is sloppy about how they make or communicate decisions. We never know for sure, so assume good faith, patiently ask them to explain, and if they are willing to do that, accept that they have shown enough judgment to own their decision.

But more than that, remember that "bikeshedding" is negatively laden but is used in situations in which it is ambiguous who has caused the problem. Thus, it's a term best avoided.

Taking On Inclusion

Jason Wong

So, you're a leader of a 5- to 30-person engineering organization. You've heard of all the benefits of diversity. You believe it's the right thing to do for your business and for society. And, you now find yourself sitting around a table with your all-male leadership team wondering how you can hire more underrepresented minorities.

First, congratulations for thinking about this now. There will be no easier time to fix your diversity problems than today. The good news is that finding diverse candidates is literally the easiest problem to solve. The bad news is that you're thinking about the wrong problem.

I've talked with enough leaders of small companies to know there's a lack of understanding of what supporting diversity truly means and how much effort it requires. Most leaders start their efforts by focusing on where to find and how to hire underrepresented minorities. But, assuming your company allows these folks to make it through the door, what happens next?

The answer: terrible things. Having been through transforming an almost all-male engineering team into a diverse organization, I can tell you that our workplaces are meat grinders. By default, they are wildly unsafe places for underrepresented minorities (URMs). URMs on average get paid less than their white male counterparts (*https://oreil.ly/xsA8A*), are promoted less frequently (*https://oreil.ly/MOrgL*), and experience high degrees of harassment (*https://nyti.ms/2E3kKAd*). If you're lucky, it comes in the form of casual jokes or comments. If you're like most, there are far more serious acts being committed. And, to truly reap the benefits of diversity, you're going to need to address these issues head on.

When I prepare engineering leaders for this work, I talk about three inflection points that I've found to be common stumbling points.

The first is *not complicit to complicit*. We all like to think of ourselves as good people. Or, at least inert enough to not be actively causing harm to others. So being called out for perpetuating sexism and discrimination is really tough to take in. What's important to recognize is that the forces that lead to our biases are systemic. We are all complicit in some way, even the most fervent supporters of diversity and inclusion. And, similar to the stages of grief, getting to acceptance is key to moving forward. So, the question isn't whether we are complicit, but how complicit are we and what are we going to do now that we're aware?

The second inflection point is *believing in the lived experiences of others*. After we open ourselves up to hearing from different voices, the next phase is actually believing what we're hearing. Because we live in a world filled with bias, two people can do the exact same thing and end up with very different outcomes. Marginalized people who report discrimination often find that doing so negatively affects their careers (*https://oreil.ly/boXbD*). When URMs raise issues, they often are labeled complainers or trouble-makers, whereas those they complain about have historically seen no consequences or repercussions for their actions. Defaulting to believing the lived experiences of others ensures you can expose and address the issues of inequity in your workplace.

Finally, *spending time and money*. Talk is cheap. When someone comes to you and asks for $25,000 for an employee resource group program or to divert engineering for the next week to remove master/slave terminology from your codebase, you will hesitate. And the question is this: will you actually follow through?

The thing about these inflection points is that you will encounter them over and over again. You will accept one aspect of your complicitness and then come across another. You will begin to believe one set of lived experiences while still being incredulous of someone else's. You will hear how your words and actions (or inactions!) are contributing to the problem and not the solution. You will not believe people when they tell you this. You will need to accept that they are probably right. This work is difficult. And tiring. And frustrating. But if you're successful, not only will your business be far more likely to succeed, but you will have created a new norm—one in which all identities are welcome and where equitable treatment and fair outcomes prevail.

Team Stability Matters

Bill Horvath

If you're running an engineering department, you may find yourself tempted to move people around between teams to address fluctuations in demand from customers and other business stakeholders. While we welcome changing requirements, even late in development (*https://agilemanifesto.org/princi ples.html*), changing team composition to address them is a mistake.

Why?

Teams that stay together are better, in all kinds of measurable ways.

All else being equal, a team with stable membership will perform better over time. And there's lots of empirical data to back this up: studies show team stability leads to high performance, predictable velocity (*https://oreil.ly/ 9grqa*), and outcome quality (*https://oreil.ly/Fk4ms*), just to name a few.

Team performance data only has meaning when the team membership doesn't change.

Some software development teams measure their performance in terms of velocity; others use measures of code quality (such as bugs that escaped into production); still others use even simpler gauges, such as number of features delivered. But regardless of the data that's collected, *the more the team's membership changes, the less meaningful the data becomes, because the unit of measurement has changed.* A stable team's work metrics have meaning *because* the team is stable.

There's an interactive effect between team stability and product owner effectiveness.

In an Agile shop, the product owner constructs work items with the capabilities and past performance of the team in mind. Their knowledge of the team can have a profound impact on how the product owner writes the work items, and where they place them in the backlog. As the product owner's knowledge of the team grows, their ability to write consistently sized work items that the team can easily estimate and execute becomes better and better.

Their performance becomes stable, which means it's predictable.

Predictable performance means it's easier to roadmap features, especially with a well-maintained backlog. If several sprints-worth of stories at the top of the backlog are sized, it's easy to see the impact that changing the order or adding new features will have on the product roadmap.

Psychological safety is positively correlated with team effectiveness and negatively correlated with membership changes.

Recent research (*https://oreil.ly/Ea19u*) shows a strong negative correlation between team tenure diversity (i.e., variability in how long the members have been on the team), and team psychological safety, which predicts team effectiveness (*https://oreil.ly/tF8NA*). In other words, the more a team changes, the less likely it is that its members will trust one another, and the greater the odds that they'll lose effectiveness as a result.

A Possible Solution to Pressure

Depending on the discretion you're granted, you might not be able to directly resist stakeholder demands to move people between teams in order to meet deadlines. Aside from pointing out the one-month birth fallacy (*https://oreil.ly/kV9wl*), there are other approaches that you might consider. For example, you might have a roaming "firefighter" team whose role is to acquire knowledge across products and supplement teams under pressure by pulling tickets from their backlog that are relatively independent of the rest of pressured-team's work. This kind of approach works particularly well when the department has well-documented definitions of done that include stringent quality-control measures such as automated testing and code reviews of every commit.

Regardless of your chosen approach, you'll find it well worth your while to defend the stability of your development teams—their psychological safety (and perhaps yours) depends on it.

Three Questions to Avoid, and Three Questions to Ask During an Interview

Lorenz Cheung

When I was first promoted to technical manager and started hiring, I loved asking "tough" questions. One of my favorites was, "What's your three strengths and three weaknesses." Most of the candidates would struggle and couldn't fully answer the question and performed poorly. I thought I did the smart thing and revealed the true characters of the interviewees, until one time I got an answer: "My weakness is that I am afraid of coldness." That's the moment when I knew I screwed up. Not only had I been asking a pointless question, I encouraged people to give "fake" scripted answers. This question especially filtered out the more technical people and kept the people that do only the talking and not much of the doing. Thus, this was the first question I learned to avoid.

Another question I loved to ask was, "Tell me what you do in this scenario." This question seems common enough and quite sensible; we can see how developers would react in the tough situation. The issue is that this is a virtual situation, does not really relate to real-life situation, and does not dig deeper into the usual role and responsibilities of the individual. People can just tell the story of someone else. Most would not give the real answer at work: "I would google it." Again, this question seems great at first, but I learned to stop asking.

The last one is the famous Google IQ questions like, "Estimate the number of tennis balls that can fit into a plane." It seems really great—Google used it, so it must be good, right? The question allows us to the gauge the IQ and creativity of an individual. What could be the issue? The problem is, though, that how high an individual's IQ is or how smart they are has nothing to do with on-the-job performance. Google has conducted the internal research and has stopped using the question. Quite often we are not looking for the smartest person: we are looking for the person who has the skill and experience as well as company and culture fit.

So, we've covered three questions to avoid. What three questions should we ask, then?

What have you learned in the past six months?
>Good engineers continue to learn about technology. In this question, we are interested to know whether the candidate has a growth mindset. We are interested to know whether the individual takes time to learn, either about work or personally, be it a new language or a new skill set. It has been discovered that individuals with a growth mindset are more likely to take on challenges and learn from them, therefore increasing their abilities and achievement.

Tell me about a time when you failed and what you learned from that?
>This one is related to the growth mindset and learning as well. We are interested to know how the individual reacts to failures and learns from mistakes. Mistakes and failure are a part of the life of engineers; the more interesting bit is how we deal with them. We are also asking in an attempt to probe the integrity and courage of the engineer. We can follow up and ask the individual about a past conflict and how they would handle it now. Again, we probe into real-life experience and check their working style. With this one, we are interested to know about the more stressful experience the candidate has experienced

Do you have the skills, expertise, and experience to perform the job?
>Here we drill into details. We dig into the actual work done by the individual. We ask developers to show us their work, tell us how they build the mobile, web, AI, API or technical components, worked out through each step. Most important, we ask them what they do as an individual to help the team. For development, we are asking for technical questions related to that environment: object-oriented design, design patterns, code review, DevOps, different type of testings, security, scaling, Agile. And so on. We ask the candidate for real-life experience, and at the same time we are probing their presentation and communication skills. Last but not least, we follow up with a real programing test, either at the venue or a remote location through online tools so that developer can be in the most comfortable environment and think properly.

Three Ways to Be the Manager Your Report Needs

Duretti Hirpa

I've worked as a software developer my whole career—and I've worked everywhere from small mom-and-pop shops, to agencies, to companies going through hypergrowth. At one company, I had a new manager every quarter. Having a slew of managers in a short timeframe trained my eye: I can spot a s--- manager in fewer than three one-on-ones, and I know what the decent ones try to do. I've become obsessed with quickly and accurately unveiling a bad manager and identifying which traits separate the bad ones from the good ones. Let me tell you what I know.

Lesson One: One-on-Ones

As a manager, you've probably heard that the one-on-one (the weekly meeting where you spend between 30 minutes to an hour with your report) is sacrosanct. A good manager knows this; a great manager lives this. Bad managers leave you waiting in the agreed upon room, eventually messaging some flavor of, "oh, did you need the 1:1 this week?" If your report (like me) has been socialized to be agreeable and consents to skipping, you will have set a dangerous precedent. This is the first fracture.

It's possible that you might not know *why* skipping a one-on-one is important, so let me tell it to you from one of your own. Marc Hedlund, former vice president of engineering at Etsy and Stripe, says, "Regular one-on-ones are like oil changes; if you skip them, plan to get stranded on the side of the highway at the worst possible time." A one-on-one is an investment in the future. It's a seed you plant, it's regular exercise, it's eight hours of sleep a night.

If you ask to skip, you're sending a message. You're saying to your report, "You're not important to me this week." Like most subversive things that become easier the more you do it, skipping one-on-ones goes from, "You're not important to me this week," to, "You're not important to me," to, "You're not important." Don't do this. Your one-on-ones should be so regular that if one is canceled, your report thinks something happened to you.

Lesson Two: Follow Through

The most helpful advice I can give anyone (and it works in a variety of contexts) is to follow through. What is trust if not consistency over time? Be consistent, show up. Show up physically to your one-on-ones. But, more crucial, *show up* for your report. Did they ask you a question? Great, that's an assignment. Go find out what you can tell them. If you can't tell them anything, that's fine—but close the loop. Otherwise, you're unreliable; a black-hole where my requests go to die. For you to do your job well, I need to trust you. With each successful closing of a loop, you build trust with me, your report. Every closed loop you miss? You teach me that you're not someone I can rely on, and with enough time, I'll treat you accordingly.

Lesson Three: Avoid Causing Anxiety

As your report, I'm intensely aware of you. I'm lurking on your calendar, I'm noticing how and where you spend your time, what you're doing, and with who. I'm talking to your other reports about you. We strategize. That's why when you deviate from your pattern, we'll know. If you ask us whether we have time to chat or if a calendar event shows up with no context, we'll worry (honestly? we think we're getting fired—no matter our standing in the company). Forgetting to set context strikes anxiety into the hearts of your reports —and you're not heartless, are you? Hopefully not, else you wouldn't have chosen a profession trafficking in other people's careers. Remember: you control our careers and our financial prospects. A bad manager forgets this. A good one never does.

Caring is what separates a good manager from a bad one. I get it: life is easier when you *don't* care, when you *don't* put in the effort. But, if you're going to do this job, and do it well? Caring is the baseline. Being a great manager is not about amassing influence or power or authority. It's about showing up, daily, in small steady ways. When you build up your reports, you enable them to build, too. That's what they'll remember; not the specifics of every project, but the way you, their manager, cared about them. That's something that'll last longer than any tenure at any company.

We can build so much more than software when we care.

To Code or Not to Code

Ben Edmunds

If you've been an engineering manager for more than a few minutes, you've likely received the advice, "Stop coding!" You're a manager now, the value you bring to your team isn't in the code you produce. Or maybe you've received the exact opposite advice, "Always be coding!" You're a manager now, you don't want to lose your technical chops. Neither of these work well in my experience. Let me begin by explaining my own journey.

Early in my management career I subscribed to the idea that you should continue coding. I was as active as ever, shipping as often as I did before, and trying to keep the same personal measures of success. This led to me working nonstop. I was attempting to fulfill my management duties during the day, then code all night. This caused alternating resentments. Either I would resent managing because it was interfering with coding, or I would resent coding because I had something I needed to handle on the management side. This was a horrible disservice to my team and to myself. I was a burned-out engineer and a horrible manager.

From here I swung to the other side. I attempted to stop coding. When I was coding, I saw it as a failure. It was a sign of my inability to delegate or plan well. This led to a constant state of frustration in myself and even more pressure on my team. I also started to see the effects of losing my technical edge and became removed from the constraints my team was working within.

Finally, I settled into a workable balance between these two extremes. I hope my experience can help you find balance, as well. Here's what works for me, in priority order:

Management
> This includes one-on-ones, planning, interfacing with other teams, and being available to your team.

Code reviews
> This keeps me in the loop on what we're shipping.

Architecting

Performed with other engineers, I'm a sounding board and provide guidance.

Fixing bugs

This is the majority of my coding now. I no longer have large blocks of focused time but often have 30- to 60-minute blocks. It's a great way to stay up to date on the day-to-day issues that your team is facing. It keeps you in touch with your codebases and it helps take some pressure off your team.

Internal tools and automation

I try to identify tools that streamline internal processes or things that can be automated to save time. Often working it at a slow pace, as I get time. It might take me weeks to finish but that's ok as long as it's not urgent.

My priorities might not work for you as is; you'll need to define your own. Here's how I recommend starting to explore this.

First, being a manager is your top priority. Not empowering your team to be the best they can be is causing more damage than you not writing as much code. A team of people will always be more productive than you'll ever be. With that in mind, look at what responsibilities you have as a manager to determine what technical work fits within those constraints. It might be architecture, it might be writing documentation or requirements, it could be small features or fixing bugs. There could also be some subset of these things. The important part is being realistic with yourself on what you can do and how you can do those things while still putting your team's needs first.

Next, redefine what success looks like for yourself. As managers, we don't get the constant dopamine hit of closing tickets and shipping code like we did as engineers. That's ok. Don't try to continue to feed your self-worth with those metrics. Write down a list of goals for your average week that includes both management and technical items. That might include things like one-on-ones, team meetings, or scheduling; along with planning the architecture for the next big feature and preforming code reviews.

Finally, set your expectations and communicate them to your team and elsewhere. Ensure that everyone knows where your priorities are and why. This prevents miscommunication over why you aren't handling things others might expect from you. Write these priorities down in a clear way that you can reference.

Most of all, understand that day-to-day tasks aren't set in stone. As a manager you need to be fluid and move to the issues that have the highest priority in the moment. Each day will be different from the last. Some days are for doing, some days are for talking and thinking, and some days are for fighting fires.

To Code or Not to Code

Transparency Takes More Than an Open Door

Seth Dobbs

"I have an open-door policy," is a claim I often hear from managers and leaders. It's a statement that is meant to sound positive and make the speaker seem approachable, but I'm not sure that this is always the case. Don't get me wrong, the *intent* behind this notion is positive and worth understanding, but my sense is that if you're bragging about the "policy" and not the results, something might be amiss.

To begin, for many of us in leadership positions, stating, "I have an open door, come in any time!" is easier said than done. Our jobs as leaders and managers often require us to be heads down in a problem, spend time in deep strategic thinking, and to fill our calendars with planned interactions. Given that, how easy is it for your team to *actually* find time with you? Can people really walk in throughout the day and chat?

Also, how comfortable are your people in taking up your time? Role power will naturally make people hesitant to speak to you no matter how much you tout your open door. Even people who are naturally approachable can suffer from this because people on your teams might feel that no matter what you say, you are too busy to actually listen to them. And when you have role power it's really easy to inadvertently imply that you're too busy.

How do you react when people walk in the door and tell you something you don't want to hear? If you are dismissive, unreceptive, or, worse, aggressive, how often do you expect people to come back? Do you actively listen and even empathize? Do you just nod your head, say, "Thanks," and let them walk away? Again, due to role power, people might fear the reaction of their leaders for adverse opinions, so it takes more than just saying you have an open door to get meaningful input.

I feel that sometimes we encourage feedback on the belief that we're mostly going to hear positive things or minor changes that we already had in mind and the feedback we receive will reinforce it. However, if you're not truly ready to hear contrary opinions and criticism, be careful what you encourage!

Given the challenges in actually getting people through your door and having meaningful conversations, I have to wonder what claiming an "open door" actually accomplishes. My fear is that we can have the illusion of knowing what's going on. It's easy to claim, "No one has come in and complained," and therefore assume everything is fine, but that's likely not true. Your teams are always talking about something. That you not hearing it doesn't mean it isn't happening.

A Better Way

If we take a step back and look at *why* someone might have a positively intentioned open-door policy, I'd say there are a couple key goals: fostering communication and collaboration, and knowing how your people are doing. Again, I'd offer that simply having an open door or talking about having an open door will accomplish these.

A good leader doesn't wait for people to come to them. We should actively seek out feedback instead of waiting for it to trickle your way. We need to build trusting relationships (*https://oreil.ly/VYIJp*) so that our people feel like they truly can talk to us. Getting there requires reciprocal transparency. In other words, we can't expect people to tell us everything on their minds if we keep the reasoning behind all of our decision-making a secret. It requires being able to hear things that make us uncomfortable, that might make us question whether we're actually doing a good job.

Also, depending on the size of your organization, you might need intermediaries who are trusted and can bring information to you. Then, if you hear of a problem, don't just say, "Let them know they can talk to me." You'll run into the same issues associated with an open door: people think you're too busy (and maybe you are). Instead, seek out the people and let them know you are interested in learning more.

Put simply, these are the key ingredients to having open communication across your team:

- Build relationships
- Seek feedback

- Develop trust
- Be open about mistakes
- Take action!

This last point is what makes the relationship really work. If people see that positive changes come from providing feedback, they are more likely to speak up again. This is a good thing.

Finally, in an even moderately large organization you'll need intermediaries, so make sure that every team member has a relationship with someone who is trusted and seeking feedback and who will bring to you concerns they can't resolve.

If we do this properly, instead of saying, "I have an open-door policy, people can come in any time," we can state that we have a close relationship with our people and can work with mutual transparency to collaborate on even the most difficult issues facing our organization.

The Triangle of Self-Organization

Andy Brandt

The idea of self-organizing teams is at the core of contemporary approaches to managing complex work. However, it's still frequently misunderstood as something anarchic, that will just happen if we let it, needing neither attention nor guidance. In reality, productive self-organization within a group, one that supports the purpose for which the group was formed and helps it transform into a team, occurs only if certain conditions are met.

The *triangle of self-organization* identifies three key conditions influencing group self-organization: *goal, rules,* and *tension.* Managing self-organizing teams is done indirectly, mostly through those three elements. Of course, this is assuming that there is no imposed structure (roles, manager), and the group is actually free to self-organize.

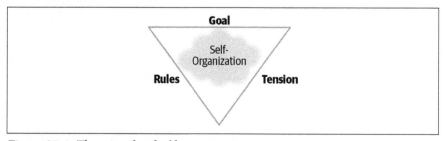

Figure 87-1. The triangle of self-organization

To self-organize, the group must have a clear *goal* that everyone is aware of. This goal shapes the process—different goals require different skills and methods. A shared goal is also the difference between a group and a team—to become a team, the group needs a goal around which to coalesce.

The goal can be implied, but it is more effective if it is openly stated. Shorter, more concise goals are easier to memorize and understand and therefore more compelling. If the group shares a physical space, it is a good idea to display the goal somewhere.

A *set of rules* the group must abide by—the shared "do's" and "don'ts"—govern how it organizes around the goal. They vary from case to case and just as the goal they can be assumed or—better—stated openly. Often, some of the rules will come from the organizational context of the group—organization's technical standards are a good example of rules that are in effect imposed on the group. The group can, and usually does, add some additional rules of its own.

Rules should be few and simple. Too many rules or rules that are complex are likely to be ignored by some or all members of the group.

Finally, *tension*—a short-term motivator and reason why the group members should expend energy in the effort to self-organize into a team, engage, and achieve the goal rather than remain passive and wait.

Usually the pressure of time creates enough tension to get the group. Sometimes, the tension can result from a challenge or a reward.

To summarize, for a group to self-organize (and become a team), three elements need to exist: a clear *goal*, understood and embraced by all in the group; a set of *rules* they will follow; and an element of *tension*, for the group members to engage now rather than wait.

The Triangle in Context

The basic triangle concentrates on short-term elements, but self-organization happens within a broader organizational context.

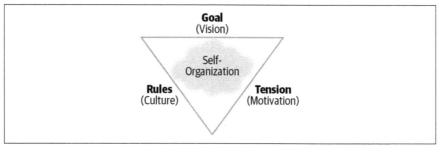

Figure 87-2.

Short-term, concise goals that the group strives to achieve should be rooted in a long-term vision. Similarly, although the tension motivates people to act now, they must be motivated to engage at all. Rules should be in line with the organizational culture.

Vision, culture, and approach to motivation are longer-term issues that each organization must take into consideration when developing self-organizing, self-managing teams. It is quite common to see companies try and fail in implementing Agile methods because they are incompatible with existing culture and vision.

Conclusion

Self-organization is a modern management tool that replaces command-and-control as a method of creating teams and guiding them to deliver desired outcomes (i.e., valuable products). To use it productively, managers and teams should be aware of three essential components needed to guide this process—goal, rules, and tension—and choose them consciously to achieve intended outcomes. Care must be taken to ensure that those are in line with existing culture, vision, and approach to motivation.

Trust Is a Powerful Leadership Tool

Seth Dobbs

"Is it better to be feared or loved?"

This is a somewhat cliched interview question for potential leaders that is intended to try and capture how a leader wants to be perceived. There are die-hard advocates of each answer as well as people who are deeply opposed to one or the other. I like to dissect this in terms of the goal of a leader, which I believe is to influence individuals, teams, and organizations to effectively deliver durable results.

Fear can certainly be a motivator to complete tasks. Team members who are afraid of some form of punishment, be it being yelled at, losing a bonus, or being fired, will absolutely be motivated to avoid that negative outcome. There are leaders who take some pride in this—that their team members fear them a little bit. Again, this can drive people forward and get them to complete tasks and meet deadlines, but if we look at the "durability" goal for leadership, this approach ultimately fails. Most people don't want to work in fear; the stress and unpleasantness of that kind of environment will lead them to find an opportunity to get out whenever they can. Even short-term results can be jeopardized because people are doing whatever they think will let them go unpunished rather than what they think is right. I've always felt that the moment someone fears losing their job is the moment they stop doing their best work.

Does that mean that it's better for a leader to be loved? In truth, team members that love their leaders are often willing to do whatever is asked, and likely on a much more durable basis than when fear-driven. But sometimes this love is based on attributes that are somewhat tangential to our work—some of us love that leader that always brings in doughnuts, that's ready with a quick joke and a pat on the back. This isn't necessarily bad, but if a leader is more focused on doing things to be loved than on delivering results, a happy team might meander through their work without a clear outcome. Also, as the saying goes, love can be blind. We can see this in the way people in the tech industry exhibit hero worship of tech leaders that we don't even work for and have a belief that they can do no wrong. At some point this is unhealthy, particularly within an organization. I know I make mistakes and I want my team to point them out to me, as unpleasant as that can be.

So, where does this leave us in terms of the initial question?

Simply that it sets us up with a false dichotomy.

If there's one thing I want my team to feel toward me, it's trust. Trust isn't easy to come by, and for a leader it goes deeper than simply being trusted that you'll do what you say. As leaders, we should be trusted that we have our clients' and organizations' best interests in mind, trusted that we have our team members' best interests in mind, trusted that our team members can come and speak to us when they have new ideas or concerns, especially if they have concerns with what we're doing. Developing this kind of trust takes work, it takes relationship building, it takes consistent active demonstration that you can be trusted in these ways.

As a leader, I personally am not looking for my team to complete tasks (which can be driven through fear) or to simply do whatever I ask (which can be motivated by love). I want my team to deliver results, I want them to grow. I want them to succeed. I want them to challenge me and one another and make all of us better at what we do. Neither fear nor love can consistently create this kind of environment. In my experience, only trust can do this.

Ultimately, cultivating this level of trust gives you the ability to more effectively influence team members and organizations, and it will drive truly durable results.

Using Six-Page Documents to Close Decisions

Ian Nowland

This chapter describes how you can use a six-page document combined with a one-hour review meeting as a mechanism to close "disagree and commit" style decisions, as I learned managing at Amazon. I have had success with using this for annual team roadmaps and trade-offs of product strategy, delivery plans, and engineering implementations.

Why Documents?

For closing a decision, a document is preferred to PowerPoint; here's why:

Clarity
> Written documentation forces the writer to clarify their thoughts before discussion and state them in a way that avoids misinterpretation.

Introvert inclusion
> Documents are more inclusive of introverts who find it difficult to speak during meetings, often because they are thinking deeply about new issues raised.

The reader owns rate of information consumption
> Written documents can be read at any pace and in any order. They can be pondered.

The full argument is seen before conversation
> Questions asked are informed by the complete picture rather than where the presenter is in the slides.

Conversation rather than dictation
It is easy for PowerPoint to become the presenter giving a speech rather than a conversation among all stakeholders.

That being said, documents come with a cost to produce and review. If all stakeholders are happy, a decision can be resolved at a whiteboard, which is preferred. It is as stakeholder groups grow larger, or decisions more contentious, that a document's benefits outweigh its costs.

Document Structure, Tone, and Format

The goal of the document is to get disparate stakeholders with different backgrounds to "disagree and commit" consensus on a decision, even when they disagree with it. It does this in three ways. The first is structurally, ensuring just as much space is spent on background as the proposal. Often, it is two pages each on general background, the specific problem, and the proposed decision to solve it. The second is tone, which needs to be "state of the world." This means that it needs to dispassionately state misses rather than be defensive or hide them. Second, disagreements on strategy need to be in the document; they need to be both explicitly stated as disagreements and have their trade-offs discussed. Finally, there's the magic of six (at most) pages of text, which is no more than you'd want to read and discuss closely in one hour. It also means not cheating, having at least 1-inch margins and 10-point font.

Getting the Body Down to Six Pages

The challenge with this format is packing the necessary information into six pages. Here is a guide:

- Reduce wordiness. For every word ask: what information is it conveying? Eliminate pointless adjectives and subjective and vague terms.
- Avoid digressions and pedantic detail. This isn't a thesis assessment.
- Prefer short lists of inarguable points to longer lists that introduce arguable minor points. Arguable minor points take space on paper, headspace of the reader, and time in the meeting.
- For background detail that might be important, use appendices. Examples include long tables, detailed graphs. Importantly, there should be no narrative text in appendices.

When you have done this and the body is still more than six pages, it means that there is too much information for a 60-minute review to come to a decision. This is often the case for large proposals when an author covers requirements, design, implementation, and roadmap. Ideally, they instead separate out areas into multiple documents and reviews. If you don't want to spend that time, that is sometimes okay; stakeholders may sometimes be fine deferring agreement on such long documents that required so much work. There is even a saying: the important work is the writing, not the reading. This falls apart, though, when not all stakeholders agree.

Meeting Structure

Here's the format:

1. Presenter brings hard copies; everyone takes one
2. First 15 minutes: They sit down and begin reading; no one talks
3. Next 25 minutes: Presenter "walks the doc," calling out section numbers, asking for comments
4. Next 15 minutes: Discussion of the decision
5. Last 5 minutes: Bring the meeting to closure

Reading during the meeting ensures that everyone reads the document as opposed to just glancing over it. That's also why a paper copy is important, so people aren't distracted. Deliberately walking through the document is also important because there is a tendency to jump to discussing the decision. You need to get there, but you want to make sure everyone in the room has had time to ask questions to understand what leads to it. To close the meeting, the document author should be clear as to whether the proposal will go forward and what will happen if not.

WELCOME, {HUMAN}!— Writing Onboarding READMEs

Cris Concepcion

Onboarding new developers is a crucial responsibility for an engineering manager. A new employee will come with a lot of energy and desire to be productive. A poor onboarding will leave them lost, frustrated, and questioning their choice. A productive onboarding can generate an amazing amount of self-sustaining momentum. In 2013, I joined Safari Books Online, and my boss, Liza, took onboarding so seriously that she went on vacation during my first week at the company.[1] But, before she left, she wrote out an onboarding document, and it was amazing.

The guide—simply a Google Docs piece titled "WELCOME, CRIS!"—listed important documents, people I should meet, and a loose set of short-, medium- and long-term plans. It was a lot of what I personally would cover with a new hire when I welcomed them to the team, but having it written down was far superior to having these points described orally. Rather than being told to do a set of tasks, and going back periodically to my manager asking for what's next, it was empowering to be given just enough structure to guide my own discovery.

The experience was powerful enough that I adopted it as I hired engineers into Safari's growing team, and coached other managers into writing their own. I've continued the practice after moving to Wayfair, and also observed with pleasure as many of my other peers have written their own Welcome

---

1 Full disclosure: we were friends before I joined the company. I knew that my onboarding coincided with her annual August vacation, and she warned and apologized to me beforehand. It was fine. We still like to joke about it.

document for their people. Below is the current structure for how I build a WELCOME, {HUMAN} document.

```
Who even is your team
- Your team members and their charter
- Your role and expectations in that role
- Where does the team's current roadmap live?
- Where does the team's pain live?

What you should be doing
- What you should focus on this week
- What you should focus on in your first 30 days
- What I hope, as your manager, will be true 90 days from now
- Here is our career ladder / review process / reasons why we fire or
  promote people.

Who should you talk to
- List of humans you'll probably talk to every day
- List of humans who can teach you important job things
- List of humans who can give you good advice or background

Additional good things to know
- Who is your onboarding buddy and explicitly state that they
  volunteered to be bothered by you with dumb questions
- Docs that you should read (getting started, faqs, how to install that
  one weird tool that breaks all the time, how all happy Gitflows are
  alike but arcane ones are arcane in their own special way, etc.)
- What Slack channels (or equivalent) you should join right now and why
- What meetings you should already have in your calendar (and I have
  failed you if I haven't invited you to them)
- New hire trainings that you should be taking (security, compliance,
  etc.)
```

Further here is what I've learned over the years of iterating on this:

- Make templates, especially if you're hiring at high volume, but personally write a unique document for each person. At the very least, the 30- and 90-day goals should be specific to the hire.

- Let your peer managers create their own versions and share with each other. They can be great reflections of how different teams and managers onboard. Borrow liberally, but don't dictate to one another.

- Identify an onboarding buddy who will mentor the newcomer and be the person they can approach for all of their questions. Always ask the onboarding buddy for feedback on how the WELCOME, {HUMAN} can be improved. They are this document's exception handler.

- Be generous when listing introductions. It's better to overwhelm them with relationships at first and let them decide which ones are important.

- Don't be surprised if some are upset that they weren't included in the introduction list. It is a sign that the document is effective. And you should include them.

- Don't make them feel like an imposter. The goals aren't a test. Remind them that they passed an interview to get here and that you tested for competency and excellence in that process. They passed the test. They deserve to be on your team. They joined you with dreams and aspirations. The goals are to help them achieve that.

What I Wished I Knew Before I Started Managing a Remote Team

Cris Concepcion

In 2013, I was hired to run a remote team for the first time. It was a transformative experience, and I learned a lot. Five years later, I joined a company that wanted me to help it hire its first remote developers and train other managers on how to support remote teams effectively, which was an interesting opportunity to consolidate what I had learned. This is an adapted version of the advice aimed equally at people joining fully remote companies as well as others taking on a remote team in a hybrid org.

The job doesn't change, but the conversations do

Remote work doesn't really change the way we work with our computers or write code. However, we need to adapt in how we collaborate and bond with one another. If you're new to working remotely, most of what you will need to work on is communication.

Your expectations for documentation will increase

When spread across time zones, not everyone on a team can make a meeting or be online when a conversation occurs in chat, so it's important to make it easy for people to catch up when they do come online. All meetings should have an agenda document. People should transcribe the conversation into the document, and most meeting documents should be shared broadly. Impromptu, important conversations in person or on hangout should be taken to chat to be captured. Expand your concept of "documentation" to conversations that are saved and memorialized.

Your meme game will level up

Nuance is difficult in text. Certainly there's ;) and ¯_(ツ)_/¯, but we all became cyborgs when Disappearing Homer and Everyone Gets A Car Oprah gave us emotions that we could not otherwise express. Successful remote teams get how memes convey wins and despair :100: times better than text.

Make time for each other

Have some one-on-ones with no agenda that are purely social. Encourage people to mention one thing they're grateful for as part of their daily standup. Share pictures of pets. Share pictures of lunch. Say good morning to one another when you start your day. Say good night when you're done. Have a team coffee break during which everybody just gets on a video conference with a beverage to chat about stuff.

It's easy for remote work to feel isolating and just be about work. To build trust and psychological safety within your team, it's essential to know who the humans are on the other end of the screen.

Having people meet each other face to face is important

I've endeavored to bring new remote teammates onsite during their first two weeks. It's worthwhile for employees to meet their managers and at least a few colleagues face to face, to form the building blocks of trust. It's also worthwhile to find occasions to have teams meet together, for instance, to retro a recently completed project or kickoff a new initiative. Getting together, being present, and intensely collaborative can be extremely powerful and is worth doing regularly with your team.

Conversely, asking people to travel is expensive

A lot of people who choose remote work do so because they prioritize flexibility at work because they might have less flexibility outside of work. Asking someone to take time away from home stresses caregiving and home responsibilities. Your teammates might be able to travel once or twice a year, but recognize their burden and make sure it's worth their sacrifice. Also consider traveling to them, and rotating who goes where.

The proper tools and manners are vital

Have a video conferencing tool that can handle a lot of concurrent users. Make sure everyone has a good headset with echo cancellation. Be disciplined about telling people to mute when they aren't talking. Use good screensharing tools, like Slack Screensharing, that allow others to take control of your screen. Using screenshots in tickets or pull requests are good. Animated gifs or HTML5 video are better.

Mixed in-person/video conference meetings is not as good as all people being on video conference

There's a stark imbalance between video conferencing and in-face communication that we haven't solved yet. If you have a quarter of your attendees for a meeting in a conference room, and three-quarters remote, it is still possible for the people in that conference room to dominate the conversation because they are not limited by duplexing technology. For a level playing field, if one person is on a video conference, everyone should be video conferencing.

Why a Good Boss Likes It When People Complain

Cate Huston

I love when people complain to me. Of course, complaining is a national past time for the British, and we don't just limit ourselves to complaining about the weather or the poor availability of good tea when traveling. Brexit has provided some strong fodder for complaining (where do we begin?) but really your average Brit can complain about anything.

But, here's why complaining is so useful to me as a manager:

It helps you find out about problems
> First and foremost, complaining is an act of trust, one that gives you, the manager, the opportunity to address the issue and channel solutions. If people don't trust you enough to complain to, you might never learn what's wrong.

It is predicated on the complainer's experience
> I read an interesting article recently that said you shouldn't give feedback, but rather focus on the experience (*https://oreil.ly/zTHjg*). This can be a really helpful way to deliver tough feedback.

> Similarly, when someone who reports to you tells you about their experience, there's probably some implicit feedback there that can help you improve as a manager. Maybe they are complaining because, for example, they are missing some context that you should have been sharing with them—and probably should be sharing with other people, too.

It shows you what they value
> People usually don't complain about things they don't care about. So, when they complain, they are likely showing you what's important to them. Do they care a lot about transparency? Delivery? The specifics of

version control? Whatever it is, you have an opportunity to understand what matters to them and why it is annoying them so much.

It helps untangle conflict

When two people on a team complain about each other, what you're hearing is two sides of a conflict. This is great! Now you have the information you need to help them resolve it. Whether it's talking them through how their actions or communication have landed on each other or identifying the values or priorities or other nerve that the situation is hitting, you can coach the complainers through the process of building a more constructive relationship. Bonus, because they both have demonstrated they trust you, you can try and use the transitive properties of trust to help them create some goodwill for each other, too.

It's an opportunity for coaching and clarity

Often when people complain, it's because they think something is out of their control. This gives us the opportunity to help them grow their circle of influence. For example, if someone complains about a peer not delivering, maybe it's an opportunity to get them to see how they can be helpful, or how they can give the peer some feedback. Maybe they complain about some company policy, and it's an opportunity to understand the broader reasons and implications so that you can help them to work within their constraints rather than resorting to blame.

It broadens your scope

We are often focused on the biggest and most urgent problems, but the minor complaints we hear today can be signs of the pressing problems of tomorrow. What can we learn from them? What can we get ahead of? Sometimes it's just a helpful reminder that the most pressing problems are not evenly distributed across the team, and can help us have a sense of perspective and progress.

It's an opportunity for empathy

When we are focused on the existential, some complaints can seem a bit like... "You're bothered by that? Really?" It might not be your biggest problem, but it is theirs, so take a deep breath, and hear them out.

Of course, sometimes complaining can become toxic. It's important that people both are and feel heard, but it's also important to keep things constructive. Recognize when complaining (including your own) is becoming toxic, set some boundaries, and escalate when necessary.

Remember, one thing that's common with "nice" people is that they give others the benefit of the doubt for far too long and are horribly annoyed by the time the person in question finally gets some sense of what's going on. Turning those small, early complaints into constructive feedback—and, if the feedback is not addressed, proper documentation—can save managers a lot of work down the road.

Why You Can't Manage Humans Like They're Software

Cate Huston

Early on at Amazon, CEO Jeff Bezos famously issued a memo about how software was to be built at the company. Teams would share their data through service interfaces, or APIs, the same way that they would share it with an outside customer. That meant that a developer on one team didn't need to know anything about how another team operated in order to integrate the product it made—that person could follow the documentation and use that product as though it were an external service. Ultimately, this ease of cooperation became extremely efficient and is what paved the way for Amazon Web Services (AWS)—a $6.7 billion business that powers huge parts of the web (including Netflix).

Georgetown University computer science professor Cal Newport recently (*https://oreil.ly/J03dU*) argued that a similar idea could be applied to humans, or the way that leaders put together teams. By defining each person's work as a collection of inputs and outputs, leaders could define communication protocols to reduce the overhead of collaboration (often measured in meetings) and allow for greater efficiency in communication across teams and more "deep work."

This is the kind of extreme stance that Newport is known for—the kind of thing that makes him well known and successful as a theoretical computer science academic and author. I learn a lot from what he writes; I never apply it to the same extent.

When I thought about this idea of "humans as APIs," I thought of the teams it's been most difficult to work with: How *nice* it would be if they could just offer an API that I could ping to find out what is going on, or a notification server to which I could subscribe in order to receive well-defined and structured priority updates. What a relief that would be.

But in the end, I don't think that humans can ever be managed like APIs. Nor would we want them to be.

APIs do have some role in human management. We don't call them APIs, of course. We call them "social norms," or "culture," or—*gasp*—processes (*https://oreil.ly/gp9Dc*). They're how we operate effectively, knowing how we get the information we need when we need it.

For example, how do you know the status of a project and what you need to do next? On my team, which organizes projects into two-week chunks called "sprints," it looks like this:

- As an individual contributor (IC): You go to the GitHub project and pull the next task from this sprint.

- As a tech lead (leading one team working on one project): You look at the overall progress of the sprint, the results of the spike (time-boxed investigation that determines approach) that will influence the next sprint, maybe start thinking about adjusting scope.

- As an engineering lead (someone who manages collections of teams rather than just an individual team): You look at the overall progress versus timeline (however you report that) and either feel good that things are on track, or start asking hard questions.

There are clear processes that determine what the *state* of things is, which means we don't need to talk about it to have a clear agreement. Questions can focus on *why* that is the state right now, how people *feel* about the state, and discrepancies between expectations and reality.

We don't just do this with technical things, but softer things, too. A stranger approached me at an event to tell me that someone had shared with her my practice of responding "have you told them?" whenever someone tells me that they've received help from someone else. Over time, the responses I got to that question changed from, "no, and I should" to "yes." Our culture changed to one of appreciating each other more actively.

Or, think about how we respect organizational hierarchy. As a manager of managers, it's tempting to ask ICs to do something "small," but it's appropriate to go to their managers and ask them first—they have context you don't (hopefully, and if not, that's a different problem), and when you go straight to the ICs, you risk overwhelming them and undermining their managers.

But can these "APIs" totally run an organization? I'm skeptical.

The fundamental limitation of human APIs in an organization is that they're great for sharing information, but they're poor for decisions. And they miss a key point—trust.

One of the most shocking and exhausting things about stepping into a leadership position for me was the sheer volume of decisions that hit me every day, and the range they encompass: The big ones (Should we hire this person? How many people should we hire? What projects should we commit to?) and the small ones (Can someone take a week off two months from now? Do I need to attend this meeting when the last one was pointless?).

There's no API for these decisions, and the only way I've found not to lose my mind is to push some of the decisions down. Does this bug merit a point release? If someone's asking me that question, probably yes, but my question back to *them* is, what makes you ask? Why do you think it might, and what is stopping you from going ahead and taking that action?

Unfortunately, there's no clear API for coaching either.

Which brings me to the final point—trust. If I ask a computer to add two and two, I can feel very confident that this task will be done to my satisfaction. If I feel it's necessary, I can add a unit test to validate it.

But the things we ask of humans are messier, more complicated, and not well defined in mathematics. If I follow the information API and learn that a project is off-track, and it's a team or lead that I trust, I will start with "how can I help?" If there's no trust there, especially when it's something we need to rely on, or this kind of thing has happened too many times before, it's tempting to start with "*What on earth is going on?*"

There's a comfort for the mathematically inclined in returning to the certainty and understanding of mathematics, to think in systems and optimize for efficiency of communication between them. These things work, up to a point, but they are too static for the messiness of humans and the chaos of growth. If we leave out trust, and we leave out developing each other, we will never scale.

Why Your Programmer Just Wants to Code

Marcus Blankenship

When I interviewed Jamie for a position at ZenTech, he seemed like an enthusiastic engineer. With solid tech skills, ideas for process and product improvement and a great team attitude, he was the obvious choice.

But, two years later, Jamie was "that guy." You know, the one who wants to code without being bothered.

I should have noticed the signs. He didn't speak up in retrospectives, he didn't contribute process or product ideas like I expected, and his "team-friendly" interactions were usually sarcastic. He often talked about technical debt, our lack of innovation, and the "stupid" decisions holding us back. An irritating "I told you so" sentiment plagued his comments and feedback.

Jamie might have thought about leaving the company. If he did, I couldn't tell. Although, I certainly wished he would have. But we were shorthanded, and I needed all the help I could get.

The result? Another cliché programmer who just wanted to code and be left alone.

People Are Shaped by Environment

Too many managers believe the problem in this scenario lies with Jamie. If he were a better employee, dedicated worker, or at least cared more, then this wouldn't have happened. Right?

Unfortunately, no.

The transition from enthusiastic programmer to polarized programmer doesn't happen overnight. But it starts sooner than you think.

The First Suggestions Matter—A Lot

How you handle ideas from new programmers sends an important signal. Good or bad, it sets the stage for what they expect. This determines whether they share more ideas in the future...or keep their mouths shut.

Sure, some ideas might not be feasible in your environment. Some might be put on the back burner to be discussed "when we're not so busy." Some ideas seem great, but they run against unspoken cultural norms.

No matter what the reason, dismissing or devaluing your programmer's ideas —especially in the first few months—is a bad move.

Damaged by all the naysaying, they'll try a few more times to present their ideas differently, aiming for a successful outcome. If they continue to feel punished, though, they'll realize that the only way to win is to not play.

Which is exactly what you don't want your programmers learning.

He will stop presenting ideas, asking to meet customers, and genuinely trying to understand the business.

Ultimately, it's a lose-lose.

The Bigger the Idea, the Bigger the Risk

Remember that your programmer is taking a risk when they offer a new idea. The bigger the idea, the bigger the risk.

Why is it a risk? Because our ideas reflect ourselves, our views, and our passions. We don't advance ideas we don't care about or that we don't think will work. We put forth our best ideas with the hope they will be received.

This requires vulnerability, which only happens if we're fairly certain we won't be humiliated. If we believe our ideas won't be accepted, we stop offering them.

Feedback About Ideas Shapes Behavior

It's only natural, then, that your programmer is reduced to doing only what brings him success: coding.

His enthusiasm for creation, innovation, and development, sadly, are lost. Perhaps it transforms into unrealistic ideas about code quality or code metrics. Their concern for market share and business health is replaced with a concern for titles and pay scales. They become more worried about how much they earn, what their title is and how they look on LinkedIn. Their enthusiasm for changing the world is replaced with nit-picking the development process.

Worst of all, though, their concern that "We aren't building the right thing" will be replaced with "We aren't building the thing right." They've learned to not give input on what is built, so they become obsessed with *how* it's built.

Your culture, for that person, has become survival of the fittest.

What's Your Onboarding Teaching?

Although you would never say this directly, your onboarding and culture might be teaching some pretty negative lessons:

> "Our company doesn't like big ideas from little people."

> "You just focus on building stuff. We'll figure out what the customer needs."

> "You are just a code monkey."

> "Why are you asking so many questions? Don't you have coding to do?"

What Is Your Real Culture?

Culture isn't the slogan on your wall, or how you describe your mission during an interview. Culture is the way people actually act and what they actually care about.

Texas A&M Professor Ifte Choudhury (*https://oreil.ly/O-_Yl*) states, "A culture is a way of life of a group of people—the behaviors, beliefs, values, and symbols that they accept, generally without thinking about them, and that are passed along by communication and imitation from one generation to the next."[1]

If you wonder what kind of culture you have, start watching how people behave. If you don't like what you see, change it. Culture isn't dictated. It's learned, modeled, and imitated. As a leader, it's your job to be worthy of imitation. Because the culture isn't Jamie's fault. It's ours—team leads, software managers, and CTOs.

So, stop blaming Jamie and start making the changes that your culture demands. The sooner, the better.

---

1 I think Choudhury might have actually drawn this material from this book: Hofstede, G. (1997). Cultures and Organizations: Software of the mind. New York: McGraw Hill.

Willpower of Leadership

Mike Fisher

Willpower is an underappreciated necessity for leadership of large projects. Almost all engineering managers will find themselves responsible for implementing a large change. In some cases, this change will be a technical or systems level change, such as migrating from datacenters to a cloud provider or a redesign to shard databases. In other cases, this change will be an organizational or process change, such as rolling out a new personnel assessment process. No matter what type of project, if the project is large or impactful enough, and the people involved have lived with the status quo long enough, there will come a point where fear and uncertainty take hold. At this point in the project, what pushes the project forward is the sheer willpower of leaders on the team. As a side note, leaders exist at all levels in the organization and being a people manager isn't a prerequisite to be a leader.

The way this fear and uncertainty often manifests itself is through a team member overcome with doubt that the project will succeed. In the cloud migration scenario, an engineer might raise concerns shortly before the cutover about something like the stability of virtual machines (VMs) under a production workload. Whereas performance could be tested and predicted, something like Mean Time Between Failure (MTBF) of VMs is difficult to test other than after going live. Although possibly a valid concern, there is no logical argument or data that can be used to calm these fears. A leader's only recourse is to push forward, mitigate risks where possible, encourage team members, reiterate the vision of the future, and lead the team. To do so requires willpower. At its essence, willpower is one's ability to resist short-term temptations in order to achieve long-term goals.

Leaders can succumb to the doubt, fear, and uncertainty that are trying to stop the forward progress of the project. Giving in to the short-term temptation to end the pain and stress will delay and possibly terminate the project. Perhaps an extreme analogy, but one that clearly paints a visual of this fear to move forward, is the historic military charge. Modern warfare has rendered this maneuver obsolete, as the last US cavalry charge took place on the Bataan Peninsula, in 1942. However, from movies and books, most of us can visualize this. At some point during the charge, the brilliant and inspiring words of the military leaders fade. Fear starts to slow forward momentum and calls the soldiers back to the safety of their barricades. The sheer willpower of the leaders kicks in, pushing them forward into uncertainty, foregoing the immediacy of safety for a place in history forever celebrating their victory.

Although hopefully our projects aren't as life and death as a military charge, as engineering managers we need to dig deep to find the willpower to push forward in the face of fear and uncertainty. Acknowledge the fear and uncertainty but focus team members on what they can do something about, such as mitigating known risks, and keep reiterating the vision of a better future.

Yes, Code Wins Arguments. But Why? And How to Be Polite About It

Joe Dunn

OK, so when to stop meeting and write some code?

This came up while working with a senior software engineer recently. He had diligently gone to the project meetings, tried to move things forward, tried to drive consensus, but things were stuck. He knew in his bones that more meetings wouldn't help, but a week of him coding a prototype would. But he didn't want to "take the project away," or appear arrogant and pushy. (All good concerns…).

What to do?

"Code wins arguments" has been around for a while. This is from the Facebook S1 filing: "Instead of debating for days whether a new idea is possible or what the best way to build something is, hackers would rather just prototype something and see what works."

Classic! "Hackers would rather…." Of course they would! No more stupid meetings, we're just going to build it and you guys can sort it out later! Cool! The implied context is an argument and the outcome is a win for the hackers —which means a defeat for somebody else.

Here's the thing though: "Code wins arguments" is shorthand for a much more subtle process. Software is a creative act. When we're thinking about building a piece of software, we don't know how it's going to turn out. We really don't. We can speculate, sketch potential structures and collective outlines of what we think we're going to build, but until we start to build it, we won't know.

The best way of putting this came from a young entrepreneur I was working with a while ago. We were staring at a design for a new product. It looked good, but something was bothering both of us. Finally, he said, "We need to build it. We don't know what it wants to be yet".

In every creative process I know, there is a balance between the fine, subtle details of the actual work, and the elegance and structure of the final goal we have in mind. They inform one another. You can analyze the structure of a Mozart symphony all you want—if you don't have Mozart's command of the details, you ain't gonna write one. And if you start a novel or a software project without a good idea of the structure, after you get about a third of the way in, you'll find yourself in a tar pit—too many possibilities, too many threads that don't tie together. A mess.

So, the phrase "Code wins arguments" is, I think, blunt engineering short-hand for "we need to go and create now, and see what this thing we're building wants to be". It's a necessary step in the creative process

It does mean that for some period, the project is no longer a team sport—it's in the hands of a few (maybe one) engineers. So, there's some letting go necessary here. The rest of the team has to understand that the product won't show itself until some code gets written.

But it's also true that the wider team isn't out of the picture forever, or loses ownership. The step after coding a prototype is getting back together, seeing what's beginning to show itself, and fit it into the wider structure of the business.

Ideally in a software company, the idea that software needs periods of "just finding out" is baked in. If so, great. "We need to go and code our way through this" is an accepted stage in the process. If not, you need to get there —change the culture, which we know takes a while, and a lot of repetition.

So how to communicate this to the team? How could the engineer I was working with get out of the jam?

Well, we can ask the Magic Question: "What do they want?" My guess is they don't want to sit in fruitless meetings for hours. My guess is that they would like the project to move forward, like, now. My guess is they don't want to lose ownership. So, communicate a solution: "in a week, I can show you a prototype that does X and we'll know where to go". Or: "in two, this feature will be up and running and we can see if anybody wants it". Time-box it, make it clear it's an exploration and that it supports the project as a whole.

"Code wins arguments" implies an argument and a defeat. "Code moves us all forward" might be a better, although less pithy, approach to bring to the work.

Software is a creative process. Sometimes it needs to tell us what it wants to be. Your development culture needs to acknowledge that.

Your Job Is Not to Be Liked

Lachlan Holmes

Write down your primary goals as an engineering manager. If one of them is "to be liked," or words to that effect, you're doing it wrong.

Your job is to get results for the business. To get stuff done. As an engineering manager, this means providing direction and motivation, removing roadblocks and pain points, and ensuring great communication in the team you are managing and among peers and departments. All in a sustainable way. Bonus points if you improve any of these areas.

Perhaps you have an alternate set of goals: communication and motivation might come under the heading of culture, or collaboration and teamwork. Not different, just variations on a theme.

But there is no explicit mention of being likeable. Of course, we want to be liked. It can make any one of your job demands easier, or be a part of fostering a fun work environment. It's also important to always be considerate of people's feelings, and maintain positive relationships with your colleagues, reports, and bosses. But while it can be helpful, being likeable shouldn't be a primary goal. If it is, you will find yourself making poor decisions and avoiding necessary conflict.

I once encountered intense resistance when I asked my teams to not use their laptops during sprint planning meetings. It was a large and diverse group, and some people wanted to code or surf when colleagues from other teams were speaking. Rather than acquiesce, I went back to the purpose of the request: making meetings more effective. When the conversation was framed around our actual goals, we were able to jointly decide on an optimal solution—mandate a representative from each group to attend, and include an open invitation for everyone else. This resulted in the lead from each team attending the meetings as well as an aspiring lead. Everyone was highly engaged, the meetings were shorter, and no one used electronic devices. Trying to make everyone happy can mean an ineffective compromise, or not reaching a decision at all. After you have consulted with any subject matter experts, don't be afraid to make a call and move on. Certainly, find out the reasons why people are opposed—it could be for good reason—but don't be frozen into inaction.

When you ask a friend to do something for you, there's a good chance they will agree because of the existing relationship. In other words, they like you. In the work setting, you can't realistically hope to be liked by everybody. The classic negotiation book *Getting To Yes* (Fisher, Ury, Patton) describes a need to separate the relationship from the problem at hand, arguing that focusing solely on the problem is necessary to achieve an optimal outcome for both parties. So, although it is true that likability can help with requests, you might be selling yourself short if you don't consider other methods of influence at your disposal. For example, suppose that you need to make a joint decision with a peer in the marketing department. Rather than relying on social influence, you can use your engineering expertise to sway your peer. The best result for the company here is a merit-based debate of the options, not a favor to a friend.

If you do not ask why an employee is acting inappropriately, you might miss a chance to make their life better. For example, raising the issue with a late arriver can be an opportunity to find out that they are getting burned out. I had an employee who was dragging his heels each day. He was a high performer, but had recently become a new parent. Rather than let things work themselves out, we talked about how it affected the team culture and performance. He told me about the stress of a long commute, resulting in low energy levels at work and at home. After the chat, I made an announcement that his hours would be offset by an hour to avoid rush hour on transit. Having this difficult conversation, and risking that the employee wouldn't like me afterward, resulted in higher performance and, in the end, he might have even liked me more.

The bottom line is, be as likeable as you want, but don't let it get in the way of your job. A former colleague has described his boss as "incompetent, but too likeable to fire." Unfortunately, multiple of his reports have left, instead.

Contributors

Adam Baratz

Adam is a director of engineering at Wayfair, where he's led product and platform teams. He's written on technology for the *Boston Globe* and *Ars Technica*

Chapter 63, *Own the Narrative*

Akash Bhalla

Akash started his career as a software developer in 2007, and over the past 12 years has been fortunate to work with various teams around the globe in organizations of varying size and purpose, from helping two-person startups in Chicago, to time spent working with UNICEF in Uganda, to working as a coach and trainer in Bangalore. Since returning to London, Akash has had an opportunity to concentrate his skills on solving some of the nontechnical and organizational/structural problems faced by technical teams. As Director of Engineering at Wefarm, he is focused on building an inclusive and rewarding culture while meeting the needs of a scaling business and organization.

Chapter 41, *How to Be Discerning Without Being Invalidating*

Chapter 79, *Six Tips for a New Manager*

Alicia Liu

Alicia has more than a decade of experience in early-stage startups, building web and mobile apps from the ground up. Alicia was the vice president of engineering at Nava, the first public-benefit corporation to be a federal prime contractor, working with US government agencies to modernize digital services and infrastructure. Previously, Alicia was the CTO of Coach.me, helping people form better habits through behavior design and personal coaching.

Chapter 46, *Interviewing Engineers: Going Beyond Technical Skills*

Amy Rich

Amy Rich is a director of engineering at Nuna, Inc. She has been a DevOps leader for more than 25 years at a variety of companies, owned her own consulting business, and written professionally on the topic of UNIX systems engineering. She loves bringing order from chaos, and her work has helped improve health care in the United States, secured the web for hundreds of millions of Firefox users, and taught two generations of computing professionals.

Chapter 29, *Focus on Growth to Improve Employee Engagement*

Andy Brandt

Andy is an experienced manager, Agile and Scrum expert (a Scrum.org PST since 2010) with more than 25 years of experience in the IT/telco industry. As a management consultant he serves organizations willing to improve their processes, efficiency, and engagement of their people.

Chapter 87, *The Triangle of Self-Organization*

Arjun Anand

Arjun is a technology leader working at BeenVerified. Outside of work, he enjoys advising startups, teaching those new to technology and entrepreneurship, building things to solve problems that he sees in day-to-day life, or dabbling with blockchain. Arjun is also an avid tennis player and gamer.

Chapter 54, *Managers and Culture*

Beau Lebens

Beau has worked natively on the web since the late 90s, with the past 10-plus years being in purely distributed/remote environments. He has managed teams ranging from three direct reports to nearly 60 cross-disciplinary folks. His approach is collaborative and transparent, and he always strives to set clear expectations for his teams. Easier said than done.

Chapter 70, *Priority Exceptions*

Ben Edmunds

Ben is CTO of an awesome company that you've never heard of by day, hacking on fun ideas by night. He is also a PHP Town Hall podcast co-host and author of *Securing PHP Apps and Securing Node Apps*.

Chapter 85, *To Code or Not to Code*

Bill Horvath

Bill is an experienced software developer and avid Agilist who is honored to be serving as a principal consultant at Improving Columbus. Prior to Improving, his most notable technical achievement was programming the first release of an electronic medical records (EMR) software system in Java and founding a company to sell it. Over the course of his career, he's studied Industrial/Organizational Psychology, worked as a consultant to Congress, and volunteered as a youth coach for the Sylvania Soccer Academy, among other things. In his spare time, he enjoys spreading ideas at tech events, making art, and mentoring up-and-coming software developers.

Chapter 82, *Team Stability Matters*

Brian Fitzpatrick

Brian is founder and CTO of Tock. In 2005, he started Google's Chicago engineering office. An open source contributor for more than 13 years, Brian was the engineering manager for several Google products, and is a member of the Apache Software Foundation, a former engineer at Apple and Collab-Net, a Subversion developer, an author of several books, and a resident of Chicago.

Chapter 68, *Political Capital and the Favor Economy*

Camille Fournier

Camille is an engineering executive and author of *The Manager's Path* (O'Reilly) as well as the editor of this collection. She is a member of the engineering leadership team at Two Sigma, overseeing the firm's platform engineering organization, and is the former CTO of Rent the Runway. Her career includes numerous technology industry contributions: work on open source software including Apache ZooKeeper, membership on the board of the ACM Queue, and serving on the founding technical oversight committee for the Cloud Native Compute Foundation. She resides in New York City with her husband and two children.

Cate Huston

Cate has spent her career working on mobile and documenting everything she learns using WordPress. She combined the two by joining Automattic, where she has led mobile, Jetpack, and web teams.

Colleen Johnson

Colleen Johnson is an enterprise Lean/Agile coach, a speaker, an author, an entrepreneur and a mother of three. She espouses the importance of saying "no" and getting more by doing less. Outside of work, she's happiest with her wild crew somewhere in the woods in Colorado.

Cris Concepcion

Cris loves building things, and lately has been more focused on building legacies composed of people rather than code. An engineering manager previously at O'Reilly Media and other startups before then, Cris is currently the Director of Engineering for the Democratic National Committee, and he learns from his people as much as he teaches them.

Dave Mangot

Dave is the author of *Mastering DevOps* (Packt). Previously, he led site reliability engineering (SRE) for the SolarWinds cloud companies. An accomplished systems engineer with over 20 years' experience, he has held positions in various organizations, from small startups to multinational corporations, such as Cable & Wireless and Salesforce, from systems administrator to architect. He has led transformations at multiple companies in operational maturity and in a deeper adherence to DevOps thinking. He enjoys time spent as a mentor, speaker, and student to many talented members of the community.

Duretti Hirpa

Duretti is a writer and senior software engineer based in San Francisco. A 10-year veteran of the technology industry, she has a humanities background and often thinks about the intersection between people and technology. Duretti likes treats, the feeling of finding the perfect animated GIF to convey your meaning, and starting more projects than she can finish.

Ian Nowland

Ian is vice president of engineering at Datadog. Prior to this, he earned his manager stripes working for Camille Fournier at Two Sigma managing their Platform Compute team and shipping the first versions of what is now called EC2 Nitro at Amazon Web Services.

Ines Sombra

Ines is a senior director of engineering at Fastly, where she spends her time helping the web go faster. Ines holds an MS in computer science and an MS

---

in information management from Washington University in Saint Louis. When she is not at work you can catch her gallivanting in wine country or trying to sneak in a nap.

Chapter 12, *Culture Is What You Do When the Unexpected Happens*

Chapter 66, *Performance Is an Ongoing Conversation*

James Turnbull

James is a CTO in residence at Microsoft. A longtime member of the open source community, James is the author of 11 technical books about engineering and software. Previously, he was CTO at Empatico and Kickstarter, vice president of engineering of Venmo, and an adviser at Docker. James likes food, wine, books, photography, and cats. He is not overly keen on long walks on the beach or holding hands.

Chapter 35, *Get Deployment Right on Day One*

Jason Wong

Jason Wong is a proven engineering leader, diversity and inclusion consultant, and doughnut enthusiast. With almost two decades of experience in building and scaling web applications, he has worked in a range of industries from academia to online media and ecommerce. He helped establish web development and administrative computing at Columbia College, led development of premium video streaming services at Yahoo! Sports, and spent seven years at Etsy leading its Infrastructure Engineering team. He currently works with engineering leaders to improve their engineering management practices and establish inclusive cultures.

Chapter 30, *Followership*

Chapter 59, *On Accountability*

Chapter 81, *Taking On Inclusion*

Jay Signorello

Jay is an experienced entrepreneur and technology leader. As cofounder and CTO, Jay and his team bootstrapped Naked Apartments into New York City's largest rentals-only platform. Naked Apartments was acquired in 2016 by Zillow Group as its fifth consumer brand. After the acquisition, Jay was promoted to vice president of engineering, overseeing three NYC-focused brands at Zillow Group (StreetEasy, Naked Apartments, and Out East).

Before Naked Apartments, Jay managed engineering teams at several start-ups, including Pepperjam (acquired by eBay) and Heavy.com.

Chapter 22, *Don't Just Evaluate Candidates on Skills*

Jean Hsu

Jean is a writer, coach, and cofounder of Co Leadership, a leadership development company with the mission to help engineers step into leadership. She spent a decade as an engineer, tech lead, and engineering manager at Google, Pulse, and Medium. Jean is passionate about sharing her people-centric leadership style with teams from small startups to larger companies.

Chapter 56, *Navigating the Bumpy Road from Engineer to Manager*

Chapter 62, *Onboarding Beyond Codelabs*

Jeff Foster

Jeff is head of product engineering at Redgate. He leads continuous improvement across engineering and is responsible for setting the technical strategy and maintaining a focus on the trends that shape our industry. He works with the tech leads and other communities of practice to relentlessly improve the way Redgate builds great software.

Chapter 19, *Don't Be the S--- Umbrella*

Chapter 67, *Physician, Heal Thyself!*

Jennifer Dyni

After having many roles on her 18-plus years on software project teams, Jennifer is currently a director of engineering with Ultimate Software. Her passion is helping teams foster highly collaborative and creative work environments while making great solutions.

Chapter 15, *Delivering Feedback*

Jeremy Wight

Jeremy is a seasoned product and engineering leader with years of experience building delightful and scalable applications. He is passionate about building teams that create products that provide tremendous value to users. He currently holds the role of vice president, product and engineering at Base, the first Software as a Service (SaaS) platform tailor-built for executive assistants.

Prior to Base, Jeremy spent nearly four years in multiple product and engineering roles at InVision (*http://invisionapp.com*). While at InVision, the teams that Jeremy led saw incredible success scaling from less than one million to more than five million users. During his tenure as senior engineering manager at InVision, he oversaw the Mobile and Third-Party Integrations teams, while their iOS app was featured in the App Store multiple times, and Atlassian (*https://www.atlassian.com*) awarded it SaaS Partner of the Year for its Confluence integration.

Chapter 10, *Connect "The What" to "The Why"*

Jesse Anderson

Jesse is a data engineer, creative engineer, and managing director of Big Data Institute. He works with companies ranging from startups to Fortune 100 companies on big data. This includes training on cutting-edge technologies like Apache Kafka, Apache Hadoop, and Apache Spark. He has taught more than 30,000 people the skills to become data engineers.

Chapter 58, *Not Everyone Wants to Be a People Manager*

Joe Dunn

Joe started his career as a software engineer, working for his first startup straight out of college in Cambridge, England. He became a manager and executive, building engineering and product groups at startups in Silicon Valley and San Francisco. He has experienced everything from being one of "three guys in a garage" building an augmented reality game, to taking a company public, to creating an early entertainment website that survived the first bubble and was successfully sold. He now coaches CEOs, executives, and technical leaders at tech companies in San Francisco..

Chapter 96, *Yes, Code Wins Arguments. But Why? And How to Be Polite About It*

Josh Tyler

Josh Tyler is Course Hero's executive vice president of engineering and design, where he has grown the team from 12 people when he joined in 2014 to more than 60 today. Before Course Hero, Josh directed software development on telepresence robots for Suitable Technologies, makers of Beam robots. He is also the author of *Building Great Software Engineering Teams: Recruiting, Hiring, and Managing Your Team from Startup to Success* (Apress,

2015). He holds an MS from Stanford and a BS from Washington University —both in computer science. Josh loves the outdoors, especially with a board attached to his feet.

Chapter 7, *Career Development for Startup Engineers*

Juan Pablo Buriticá

Juan is the vice president of engineering at *Splice* (*http://splice.com/*) where he leads a globally distributed engineering organization that is building tools and services to enable musicians to unleash their creative potential. He's spent the past 10 years building and scaling distributed engineering teams for startups and bootstrapping Latin-American open source software communities. When not in meetings, he listens to hardcore punk. He was born in Bogotá, Colombia, currently lives in New York, and loves empanadas.

Chapter 17, *Distributed Teams Are Founded on Explicit Communication Channels*

Katie Womersley

Katie is vice president of engineering at Buffer and coauthor of *Atomic Migration Strategy for Web Teams* (O'Reilly). At Buffer, she leads the engineering team focusing on crafting productive, effective teams and delivering a world-class software product. Her writing has appeared in *The Next Web*, *Inc. Magazine*, and *Fast Company*. She champions remote work and loves to help others flourish.

Chapter 18, *Do Less, Lead More*

Chapter 44, *How to Share Decisions for Strong Execution*

Kaya Thomas

Kaya is an iOS engineer at Slack on the Messaging team. She graduated from Dartmouth College with a degree in computer science and did software engineering internships at Time Inc., Intuit, and Apple. Kaya is the creator of We Read Too, a book resource app that features titles written by authors of color. Aside from coding, she writes often and has bylines in *Smashing Magazine*, *TechCrunch*, and *Fusion*. Kaya has also spoken at several conferences, such as 360iDev, try! Swift, AltConf, Tech Intersections, and AlterConf.

Chapter 43, *How to Help Your New Grad Engineer Navigate Work*

Kellan Elliott-McCrea

Kellan leads teams and teaches engineering leadership. He was previously a senior vice president at Blink Health, CTO at Etsy, and an architect at Flickr.

Chapter 28, *The Five Whys of Organizational Design*

Chapter 34, *Friday Wins and a Case Study in Ritual Design*

Kevin Stewart

Kevin is vice president of platform and data engineering at Fastly. Previously, Kevin held similar roles at Heptio, an emerging leader in the cloud native computing space, and NodeSource, where he helped create NodeSource N| Solid. Kevin was one of the original engineering leaders for Creative Cloud at Adobe, where his team built the very first service offering, Creative Cloud Assets. He has helped shape the engineering culture at a number of software companies and digital agencies by improving development and delivery practices and encouraged cross-functional teams. Although he currently resides in Seattle, Kevin is a lifelong New Yorker with dreams of relocating to a sunny island in the Caribbean. When he's not helping teams build great products, you can find Kevin spending time with his family or at the gym trying to stay (get) in shape.

Chapter 73, *Reconciliation Loops*

Lachlan Holmes

Lachlan has nearly 20 years of product development experience, with much of it in the health-care domain. He has held roles from tech lead to director of engineering, and likes to work at the intersection of technology and social contribution.

Chapter 97, *Your Job Is Not to Be Liked*

Lara Hogan

Lara is an engineering leader, coach, and consultant at Wherewithall. She is also the author of *Designing for Performance*, *Building a Device Lab*, and *Demystifying Public Speaking* (A Book Apart, 2016). Lara champions engineering management as a practice, helps people get comfortable with public speaking, and believes it's important to celebrate career achievements with donuts.

Lisa van Gelder

Lisa has been in software for almost 20 years, working in a wide range of companies from early stage startups to large media companies like the BBC and the *Guardian* newspaper. She used to debug code; now she debugs teams for a living. Lisa is currently vice president, engineering at Meetup. She is mostly powered by coffee.

Lorenz Cheung

Lorenz is a technical manager, Scrum Master, Scrum trainer, and developer.

Marcus Blankenship

Marcus believes in two ideas: every programmer deserves a great boss, and every programmer is capable of building the necessary skills to become that boss. He's worn every hat from junior developer to CTO/owner, and now he helps companies build strong engineering management practices. Marcus writes and speaks at marcusblankenship.com.

Mary Lynn Manns

Mary Lynn is a professor at the University of North Carolina, Asheville and is the coauthor of two books containing strategies for leaders of change: *Fearless Change* (2005) and *More Fearless Change* (2015). She has done

---

numerous professional presentations throughout the United States, Canada, Europe, and South America at a variety of conferences and in organizations that include Microsoft, amazon.com, Avon, and Proctor & Gamble. As a professor, Mary Lynn strives to give her students the skills that will help them to change the world.

Chapter 64, *The Path to Change: Facts and Feelings*

Mathias Meyer

Mathias is an engineering culture builder, coach, hot-sauce enthusiast, and a curious mind. He's built distributed systems as well as distributed teams. He's still trying to figure out how it all plays together.

Chapter 13, *Dealing with Uncertainty*

Chapter 45, *Improve Your Decision Making with Mental Models*

Chapter 60, *On the Elusiveness of Time in Tracking Progress*

Matthew Philip

As director of delivery at 1904labs, Matthew helps build the right teams to build the right things the right way. He is especially passionate about creating humanizing and engaging work environments.

Chapter 31, *Forecasting with Less Effort and More Accuracy*

Chapter 42, *How to Conduct an Autonomy-Support Meeting*

Mike Fisher

Mike is Etsy's chief technology officer. Prior to joining Etsy, he was the cofounder and managing partner of the consulting firm AKF Partners. Mike's career in technology has also included the roles of chief technology officer of Quigo and vice president of engineering and architecture for PayPal. He has coauthored two books on scalability and has written numerous articles on business growth. Mike is a veteran, who served as a captain and pilot in the US Army.

Chapter 26, *Fire Them!*

Chapter 51, *Manage Complexity with Diversity*

Chapter 95, *Willpower of Leadership*

Mike Pappas

Mike is the CEO and cofounder of Modulate, which develops real-time "voice skins" to enable anyone to customize their voice online. Mike graduated from MIT with a BS in physics and applied mathematics in 2014. Before cofounding Modulate, Mike spent some time at Bridgewater Associates working on cloud technology, and then joined Lola Travel (a Boston travel startup led by Paul English, a cofounder of Kayak.com) as an early employee to learn more about building a successful startup from scratch. Outside of work, his passions include philosophizing, video games, and creating experimental cocktails.

Chapter 14, *Define Your Culture Before It Defines Itself*

Ned Rockson

Ned spent the first 10 years of his career working at small companies as a software engineer on search, ads, machine learning, educational software, and social apps. He started managing people officially as a cofounder of a company and became enamored of the set of problems associated with management. He joined Amazon as a manager of engineers and quickly became a manager of managers. After one year of second-line management, Ned realized that he enjoyed working as an individual contributor much more, so he recently pivoted his career back to a senior software engineer role.

Chapter 78, *Scaling Management by Giving Up Control*

Nik Knight

As an English literature and philosophy graduate, Nik Knight is not entirely sure how she ended up in tech. However, having served time on first-line support, led multidiscipline delivery teams, and spent most of the past 20 years wrangling software releases into production, she feels at home leading technical teams. A firm believer that technology is all about solving "people" problems, she has a keen enthusiasm for DevOps culture and mindset. She also holds an EMCC Foundation Award in Coaching, and likes nothing more than bringing these strands together to help people achieve more than they think is possible. After everything is safely working as expected in production, she unwinds by applying the "fail fast" principle to yoga, child-rearing, and, occasionally, karaoke.

Chapter 11, *Continuous Kindness*

Chapter 65, *People Leave Bad Managers, Not Bad Jobs—Right?*

Patrick Pena

Patrick has spent his career applying his engineering talents to the healthcare industry. In that time, he's focused on learning and growing as an engineer, a teammate, team lead, and currently as an engineering manager. He considers himself a people gardener and coalition builder and believes in people-first leadership.

Chapter 9, *Communication as Craft*

Raquel Vélez

Raquel started playing on the web after ditching the never-going-to-happen robot revolution. She currently works at Slack Technologies, Inc. as the engineering manager of the Platform App Discovery team. Previously, she has worked at places like npm, Caltech, and NASA JPL, among others. She's fairly certain laughter and chocolate will cure almost everything. In her off time, you can find her sewing, driving fast cars, speaking, and hanging out with her hilarious husband and two silly dogs. Raquel is a coauthor of the book *Make: JavaScript Robotics*.

Chapter 6, *Career Conversations as an Engineering Manager*

Chapter 52, *Management Is a Different Set of APIs*

Rocio Delgado

Rocio is a senior engineering manager at Slack. Rocio has been a backend engineer, tech lead, and manager for more than 14 years. Previously, she was a senior engineering manager at GitHub and GE and a founding engineer at WorkMarket. She's interested in performance, scalability, resilience, distributed systems, building and growing teams, and diversity and inclusion in tech.

Chapter 69, *Prioritize Building Relationships with Your Peers*

Ron Lichty

Ron has been managing software development and product organizations for 30 years at companies of all sizes, the most recent seven years as a consulting interim vice president of engineering. His primary focus throughout: *making software development hum (http://www.ronlichty.com)*. Ron's fifth book *Managing the Unmanageable: Rules, Tools, and Insights for Managing Software People and Teams (https://oreil.ly/0Tgir)* (Addison Wesley) has been compared by many readers to programming classics *The Mythical Man-Month* and *Peopleware*. His Live Lessons: Managing Software People and Teams video training is available via O'Reilly (*https://oreil.ly/a-43z*). Ron also coauthors the periodic *Study of Product Team Performance (https://oreil.ly/WHC0T)*. In addition to taking on interim vice president of engineering roles, he coaches team leads, CTOs, and vice presidents of engineering, and trains teams and executives in Agile effectiveness.

Chapter 72, *Projects for Which Agile Is Inappropriate*

Saul Diez-Guerra

Saul started his career doing social network R&D at Telefónica, the world's 10th largest telco. After a stint working on his own education startup, he enlisted with Ampush in San Francisco, where he built ad bidding systems. A tinfoil-hat privacy nut, microtargeting finally creeped him out enough to jump back from ad-tech to ed-tech, joining Thinkful to help reinvent online education. Having earned both a BEng in Computer Science as well as a BSc in Telecommunications, Saul still learns best by breaking things.

Chapter 77, *Scale Communication Through Writing*

Seth Dobbs

Seth is CTO at Bounteous, where he sets the technology strategy for clients developing ecommerce, web, and mobile products and experiences. In addition, he drives the development of technical and leadership skills throughout the organization. Seth was named Chicago's Best Technology Manager in 2016, speaks at conferences worldwide, and is an O'Reilly OLT author.

Chapter 20, *Don't Elevate the Means Beyond the End*

Chapter 48, *Leadership Is About Responsibility, Not Authority*

Chapter 86, *Transparency Takes More Than an Open Door*

Chapter 88, *Trust Is a Powerful Leadership Tool*

Silvia Botros

Silvia is senior principal engineer helping Twilio SendGrid deliver more than 40 billion emails a month for consumer brand-names like eBay, Spotify, Airbnb, and Yelp. She is passionate about scaling both teams and datastore and enjoys finding the limits of tech. You can follow what Silvia is thinking and writing about on her Twitter feed (@dbsmasher) and her blog (blog.dbsmasher.com).

Chapter 74, *"Remote"*

Steve Heller

Steve schooled at MIT through his PhD. After becoming a communications algorithms inventor at Thinking Machines, Steve joined SunLabs, where he became a manager and then lab director. He kept up his inventing (31 patents issued) and honed his approach to leadership. Steve then founded research labs at Quanta Computers and Two Sigma Investments. Fundamentally a facilitator, Steve believes that the research culture of learning and sharing is broadly valuable.

Chapter 25, *Everyone Can Lead with Leverage*

Travis Donia

Travis has spent his career at the intersection of engineering, user experience (UX), and product in rapidly growing organizations. He's currently the CTO and head of product for Context Matters, an enterprise/life science Software as a Service (SaaS) platform that was acquired in 2017. Prior to that, Travis was the first hire at DailyVoice, where he led the engineering and product team as the site launched and scaled its consumer news network.

Chapter 4, *Building Effective Roadmaps*

Chapter 16, *Developing Communication Patterns*

Chapter 55, *Monuments and Hamburgers*

Chapter 71, *The Product Manager's Concerns*

Travis Kimmel

Travis is the CEO and cofounder of GitPrime, the leading provider of data-driven metrics for software engineering organizations. As a Y Combinator alum and former engineering leader, he is focused on helping software teams use data to become more effective and to bridge communication between engineering and the rest of the enterprise.

Chapter 8, *Communicating with Executives*

Vrashabh Irde

Vrashabh is a customer-obsessed people and software development manager. He has 11 years' experience building great products and teams, engineering management for more than six years, and a history of doing interesting things at Startups/Amazon/Oracle.

Chapter 39, *Help Yourself to Better One-on-Ones*

Will Larson

Will Larson has been an engineering leader and software engineer at technology companies of many shapes and sizes, including Yahoo!, Digg, Uber, and Stripe. He is also the author of *An Elegant Puzzle: Systems of Engineering Management* (Stripe Press, 2019).

Chapter 36, *Good Process Is Evolved, Not Designed*

Yvette Pasqua

Yvette loves leading engineering teams with a focus on continuous learning, iteration, and using data to launch software at scale. She was the CTO at Meetup, shipping software that empowers 50 million members in 190 countries to build real-life connections and communities. She led the team through a replatforming, acquisition by WeWork, and more than doubling in size. Yvette's career has included engineering leadership roles at high-growth startups and product development firms where she's led through multiple successful acquisitions and launched software to hundreds of millions of people, including leading the team that built Grindr during the first few years of Grindr's most rapid growth.

Chapter 49, *Leading Through Rapid Change Is Normal*

Chapter 57, *The New Way to Manage by Walking Around*

Index

growth opportunities, 8, 53

leadership opportunities, 51

manager's role in, 17

for new grads, 118-119

for startup engineers, 20-22

whether to enter management, 158-159

Chaleff model of followership, 80

change, leadership during, 133-135,
249-250

Cheung, Lorenz, 216-217

CI/CD (Continuous Integration/Continu-
ous Delivery), 95

clarity, 29, 70-71, 120

coding

by managers, 220

team members only wanting to code,
246-248

testing candidates in, 63

collaborative environment, creating,
136-137

communication, 27-28

(see also feedback; meetings)

channels for MBWA, 156

complaining, usefulness of, 240-242

of decision-making process and results,
120-122

discerning and encouraging attitude
for, 113-115

for distributed teams, 47-49, 194-196

during rapid change, 134

effective, guidelines for, 27-28

equality in distribution of, 191

with executives, 23-26

exerting leverage using, 66

layers of, 85-87

in meetings, ground rules for, 104-106

missing details, requesting, 88-90

patterns for, 44-46

persuasion in support of change,
172-173

of priority changes, 185-186

with product managers, 187-189

for remote teams, 237-239

scaling through persistent written
channels, 202-203

with team members, eliciting, 7

transparency in, 223-225

of "the why", 29-30

complaining, usefulness of, 240-242

complex systems, managing, 138-139

Concepcion, Cris

onboarding READMEs, 234-236

remote teams, managing, 237-239

risk budgets, 197-199

conflict resolution, 48, 147

context provider role, 52-53

Continue and Consider framework, 41

Continuous Integration/Continuous
Delivery (CI/CD), 95

culture, 38

(see also values)

APIs metaphor for, 244

defining, 38-40

evaluating, 33-34

exemplifying, 33, 146-148, 248

of inclusivity, 139

narratives within, influencing, 170-171

rituals in, 91-93

safe environments, creating, 200-201

for self-organizing teams, 190-191

D

decision-making

APIs metaphor for, 245

asking executives for, 24

bikeshedding, remedying, 209-211

communicating process and results of,
120-122

documentation for, 231-233

mental models for, 123-125

strategy for, 36

in uncertain situations, 35-37

improving, 107-109
MBWA using, 156
retrospectives of, 2-5
one-on-one-on-one meetings, 143-145
OpEx (operating expenditures), 149-151
organizational design, 74-76, 138
ownership, 160
    (see also accountability; responsibility)

P

Pappas, Mike, 38-40
partners, follower type, 81
Pasqua, Yvette
    leading rapid change, 133-135
    MBWA (management by walking
        around), 155-157
peer relationships, 183-184
performance
    measuring, team stability required for,
        214
    problems with, addressing, 176-178
performance reviews, 78, 129
persuasion in support of change, 172-173
Philip, Matthew
    autonomy-support meetings, 116-117
    forecasting, 83-84
PMs (product managers), interactions
    with, 187-189
political capital, earning and spending,
    181-182
pre-mortem exercises, 139
presentations
    to executives, 24-26
    exerting leverage in, 66
Priority Exception process, 185-186
probabilistic forecasting, 83-84
process evolution, 99-101
product features (see software develop-
    ment)
product managers (PMs), interactions
    with, 187-189

product roadmaps, 12-14
professional development
    engineering ladder for, 128-130
    plans for, 77-79
progress, tracking, 162-163
prototyping, 251-253
psychological safety, 191

R

RACI (Responsible, Accountable, Consul-
    ted, Informed) matrix, 121
READMEs
    for managers, 10-11
    for onboarding, 234-236
real-time messaging, 156
reconciliation loops, 192-193
recruiting (see hiring)
remote teams (see distributed or remote
    teams)
resources, follower type, 80
responsibility, 131-132
    (see also accountability; ownership)
    DRIs for, 7
    RACI matrix for, 121
Responsible, Accountable, Consulted,
    Informed (RACI) matrix, 121
retrospectives
    of one-on-one meetings, 2-5
    of priority exceptions, 186
    of specific time period, 135-135
return on investment (ROI), 187
RFCs (Request For Comments), 47
Rich, Amy, 77-79
risk budgets, 197-199
ritual design, 91-93
roadmaps, 12-14
Rockson, Ned, 204-205
ROI (return on investment), 187
role power, appropriate use of, 132

S

safe environments, 200-201

scaling
    communication, 85, 202-203
    management, 204-205
    onboarding, 168

scheduling
    priority exceptions, 185-186
    product manager's concerns with, 188
    timeline for change, 133-135

scope of control, 67

scope of influence, 67

self-care for managers, 179-180

self-healing systems, 192-193

self-organizing teams, 190-191, 226-228

servant leaders, managers as, 116-117, 191

shame, as negative motivator, 201

Signorello, Jay, 58-59

Slack, 156

software development
    budgets for, 149-151
    bugs, handling, 188
    cost and ROI of, 187
    deployment system for, 94-98
    estimating, 83-84, 162
    feature choices, plans for, 13
    feature delivery, managing, 60-61
    features, rolling out, 13
    layers of communication for, 85
    priorities changing during, 185-186
    prototyping, when and how to use,
        251-253
    reconciliation loops, 192-193
    time requirements for, 15-16
    tracking progress, 162-163
    vague requirements for, avoiding,
        88-90

Sombra, Ines
    culture, 33-34
    performance problems, addressing,
        176-178

Sprint Reviews (see Friday Wins)

standup meetings, 102-103

startup companies, career development at,
    20-22

Stewart, Kevin, 192-193

strategic objectives, 13

strategy, as communication layer, 86

success
    of managers, indicators of, 6-9
    of remote teams, factors in, 194

synchronous communication channels, 48

T

tactics and process, as communication
    layer, 86

team #1, peers as, 183

team members
    changing jobs, reasons for, 174-175
    communication with (see communica-
        tion; feedback)
    exerting leverage, 65
    firing, 68-69
    follower types of, 80-82
    guidelines for one-on-one meetings,
        107-109
    handoffs to a new manager, 143-145
    hiring (see hiring)
    managing as APIs, 243-245
    new grads, helping, 118-119
    onboarding, 164-166, 167-169, 234-236
    only wanting to code, reasons for,
        246-248
    performance problems, addressing,
        176-178
    managing as APIs, 140-142
    productivity of, 60-61
    professional growth of (see career
        development; professional develop-
        ment)
    remote (see distributed or remote
        teams)

sharing decisions, 120-122

Wong, Jason

    diversity and inclusivity, 212-213

    followership, 80-82

working relationships

    kindness in, importance of, 31-32

    respectful treatment in, 7

About the Editor

Camille Fournier is an engineering executive and author of *The Manager's Path* (O'Reilly) as well as the editor of this collection. She is a member of the engineering leadership team at Two Sigma, overseeing the firm's platform engineering organization, and is the former CTO of Rent the Runway. Her career includes numerous technology industry contributions: work on open source software, including Apache ZooKeeper, membership on the board of the ACM Queue, and serving on the founding technical oversight committee for the Cloud Native Compute Foundation. She resides in New York City with her husband and two children.